The Institute of Chartered Accountants in England and Wales

PRINCIPLES OF TAXATION
FA2014

For exams from 2015

Question Bank

www.icaew.com

ICAEW

Principles of Taxation
The Institute of Chartered Accountants in England and Wales

ISBN: 978-0-85760-986-1

Previous ISBN: 978-0-85760-821-5

First edition 2007

Ninth edition 2014

British Library Cataloguing-in-Publication Data
A catalogue record for this book is available from the British Library

Printed in the United Kingdom by Polestar Wheatons

Polestar Wheatons
Hennock Road
Marsh Barton
Exeter
EX2 8RP

Your learning materials are printed on paper obtained from traceable sustainable sources.

Contents

Title	Page	
	Questions	Answers
1. Ethics	3	115
2. Introduction to taxation	7	117
3. Introduction to income tax	9	119
4. Employment income	15	125
5. Trading profits	23	131
6. Capital allowances	31	135
7. Trading profits – basis of assessment	37	139
8. National insurance contributions	43	145
9. Capital gains tax – individuals	47	147
10. Corporation tax	55	153
11. Value added tax	75	165
12. Valued added tax: further aspects	93	173
13. Administration of tax	99	175
Tax tables FA2014	185	

Question Bank

Your exam will consist of 50 questions with equal marks, together adding up to 100 marks. You should complete them all.

The questions are of four types:

- **Multiple choice** – select 1 from 4 options A, B, C or D (see Chapter 2 Q1)

- **Multiple response** – select 2 or 3 responses from 4 or more options (see Chapter 3 Q9)

- **Multi-part multiple choice** – select 1 from 2 or 3 options, for two or more question parts (see Chapter 2 Q2)

- **Numeric entry** – rounded to the nearest pound (£) (see Chapter 3 Q2)

Chapter 1: Ethics

1 Select which of the following options is **not** a fundamental principle of the IESBA Code of Ethics.

   A   Professional behaviour
   B   Professional intellect
   C   Integrity
   D   Objectivity
   E   Confidentiality
LO 1f

2 William, a Chartered Accountant, is being threatened by his client, James. James is threatening to harm William's family if William refuses to launder money for him.

   Select which one of the following options correctly identifies the type of threat William is experiencing according to the IESBA Code of Ethics.

   A   Self-interest threat
   B   Self-review threat
   C   Advocacy threat
   D   Familiarity threat
   E   Intimidation threat
LO 1f

3 Roger is a Chartered Accountant and is married to Jennifer, who is also his client. Jennifer runs an assortment of businesses on behalf of her father. Roger knows that Jennifer comes from a wealthy criminal family. However, Roger has never queried the funding of Jennifer's businesses as he trusts her implicitly.

   Select which **two** of the following options correctly identify the types of threat Roger is experiencing according to the IESBA Code of Ethics.

   A   Self-interest threat
   B   Self-review threat
   C   Advocacy threat
   D   Familiarity threat
   E   Intimidation threat
LO 1f

4 Florence, a Chartered Accountant, knows that a client, Freddy, has financed his business using the proceeds of his criminal activities for a number of years. Florence has not reported this and has instead accepted substantial payments from Freddy which are ten times her normal fee for comparable work. Florence's friend has given her the following advice.

   (i)   Freddy is laundering money through his business and as Florence is aware of this she is required to disclose it to the proper authorities.

   (ii) Florence should discuss her decision to go to the authorities with Freddy.

   (iii) Florence may be guilty of money-laundering offences as she has assisted Freddy in concealing the proceeds of crime.

   (iv) Florence was justified in increasing her fee for such risky work.

   Select one of the following options which identifies which of the friend's statements are correct.

   A   (i) only
   B   (i) and (ii) only
   C   (i) and (iii) only
   D   (i), (iii) and (iv) only
LO 1g

5   Iqmal is a Chartered Accountant who has just become suspicious that a client is engaged in money laundering.

Iqmal should report this to the firm's Money Laundering Reporting Officer

A   Once there is sufficient proof of money laundering

B   Now

Any Suspicious Activity Report would be made by.

C   Iqmal

D   The firm's Money Laundering Reporting Officer   LO 1g

6   Select which of the following would be offences under UK anti-money laundering legislation:

(i)   An accountant alerting a money launderer that a report has been made to the NCA.

(ii)   An accountant failing to report knowledge of a client's money-laundering activities.

(iii)   A taxpayer underpaying tax as the result of a deliberate omission from their tax return.

(iv)   A taxpayer underpaying tax as the result of an innocent error from their tax return.

(v)   The act of tax avoidance.

A   All of them
B   (i) to (iii) only
C   (ii) and (iii) only
D   (ii), (iii) and (v) only   LO 1g

7   Which of the following is **not** one of the factors for consideration given in the framework for ethical conflict resolution in the ICAEW Code?

A   Ethical issues involved
B   Alternative courses of action
C   Timescale involved
D   Relevant parties   LO 1f

8   Identify in the following scenarios whether the professional accountant is committing an offence under the anti-money laundering legislation.

    Steven accepts payment from a client in relation to work performed in preparing his personal tax return. The fee is a percentage of the reduction in the tax payable based on the previous year. Steven strongly suspects that the client has failed to disclose all sources of income. He later discovers this to be the case.

    A   Offence committed by Steven

    B   No offence committed by Steven

    Trevor suspected that a client of his has been receiving income through the operation of a criminal cartel. He reported this to his firm's Money Laundering Reporting Officer (MLRO), but has not heard anything else from the MLRO. Trevor later approaches the client to advise him of his suspicions and that the firm may have to report this to the authorities.

    C   Offence committed by Trevor

    D   No offence committed by Trevor   LO 1g

9   A threat to the fundamental principles may occur when a professional accountant promotes a particular opinion, compromising subsequent objectivity. This category of threat is known as

    A   Self-interest threat
    B   Self-review threat
    C   Advocacy threat
    D   Familiarity threat   LO 1f

10 Lauren is unhappy with an explanation given to her by a client in relation to the current year's accounts. If she accepts the explanation and submits the accounts to HMRC she feels that this will compromise the principle of integrity.

    Which of the following factors is she **not** required to consider in resolving the ethical conflict?

    A   The facts that she has uncovered
    B   The relationship that her firm has with the client
    C   The client's internal procedures
    D   Alternative courses of action   LO 1f

11 Mr Blythe is tendering for the some consultancy work. The same work has also been tendered for by Comp Partners, the accountancy firm which prepares Mr Blythe's tax returns.

    The ethics partner at Comp Partners concludes that the threat from this conflict of interest cannot be acceptably reduced.

    According to the ICAEW Code, select which of the following would be an acceptable course of action for Comp Partners.

    A   Inform My Blythe of the conflict and notify him that Comp Partners is ceasing to act for him

    B   Inform Mr Blythe of the conflict and obtain his written consent to continue to act for him

    C   Inform Mr Blythe of the conflict and continue to act for him

    D   Continue to act for Mr Blythe and keep the conflict confidential   LO 1g

12 Toby is a sole trader. Which of the following actions by Toby is not an example of tax evasion?

    A   Claiming £2,000 of personal expenses through the business

    B   Omitting to record £500 of cash sales

    C   Deliberately postponing the sale of some shares from 5 April until 6 April so that he can use the following year's annual exempt amount to reduce his capital gains tax

    D   Overestimating the value of some property donated to charity   LO 1g

Chapter 2: Introduction to taxation

1   Select which one of the following items is **never** a source of UK tax law.

    A   The annual Finance Act
    B   HMRC statements of practice
    C   Case law
    D   Statutory instruments   LO 1e

2   Pauline used to earn £20,000 and paid £3,000 in income tax per annum. She has recently received a substantial pay rise and now earns £50,000. Her revised income tax is £10,000.

Select which of the following options correctly defines the principle on which this tax system is based.

    A   Progressive taxation
    B   Regressive taxation

Select which of the following options correctly classifies national insurance contributions.

    C   Direct tax
    D   Indirect tax   LO 1a

3   A government is considering abolishing the current VAT rules on all food bought in supermarkets (but not any other shop) and replacing it with the following form of taxation. Each item bought in the supermarket will be subject to a levy of £0.75. In other words a person who purchases 10 items of any value will pay £7.50 in tax.

Select which of the following options correctly identifies the principle behind the proposed system.

    A   Ability to pay principle
    B   Value principle
    C   Unit principle
    D   Neutrality principle   LO 1a

4   Select which of the following options correctly identifies a source of tax law.

    A   The Budget
    B   Statutory instruments
    C   HMRC extra-statutory concessions
    D   HMRC statements of practice   LO 1e

5   Diana is an individual who does not have a trade or business of any kind. Diana is an employee earning £30,000 per year and a shareholder in Firm Ltd. Diana has heard that the following taxes exist in the UK and is unsure which of them she pays personally:

(i)   Capital gains tax
(ii) Corporation tax
(iii) Income tax
(iv) National insurance contributions
(v)   Value added tax

Select which of the following options correctly identifies which taxes Diana could or does suffer personally.

A   All of them
B   (i), (iii) and (iv) only
C   (i), (iii), (iv) and (v) only
D   (i), (ii), (iii) and (iv) only   LO 1d

6   Select which of the following are functions carried out by HMRC.

(i)   Collect and administer direct taxes
(ii) Collect and administer indirect taxes
(iii) Pay and administer child support payments
(iv) Collect repayments of student loans
(v)   Pay and administer the state pension

A   (i) and (ii) only
B   (i), (ii) and (iii) only
C   (i), (ii), and (iv) only
D   (i), (ii), (iii) and (v) only   LO 1d

1   In addition to his salary of £24,000, Aaron received the following income in 2014/15:

	£
Interest received from a NISA	200
Interest received on National Savings & Investment Direct Saver Account	64
Income tax repayment interest	25

His net income for the year is

A   £24,025
B   £24,289
C   £24,064
D   £24,200   LO 3a

2   Patrick is single and was born on 17 March 1938. His net income for 2014/15 is £27,800.

His personal allowance for 2014/15 is £ [   ]

Enter a whole number WITHOUT the £ sign   LO 3b

3   Mackenzie is self employed and has trading profits assessable in 2014/15 of £35,565. During 2014/15 Mackenzie also received gross building society interest of £100.

What is Mackenzie's total income tax liability for 2014/15? £ [   ]

Enter a whole number WITHOUT the £ sign   LO 3i

4   William, now aged 81, married Grainne, now aged 71, on 10 December 2005. In 2014/15 William received income from his pension of £7,000. For many years Grainne has run a small shop and her business has made adjusted trading profits of £18,000 for 2014/15. The couple have no other sources of income.

The married couples allowance due to the couple for 2014/15 will initially be

A   Given to William
B   Given to Grainne
C   Shared between them equally

The allowance due to the couple to give relief at 10% is

A   £3,140
B   £10,000
C   £8,165   LO 3b

5   During 2014/15 Kael had earnings of £43,915 from his employer, from which PAYE of £6,805 had been deducted. His only other source of income was a dividend received of £1,080. He also paid £720 as a Gift Aid donation to his son's school (a registered charity).

Select which of the following represents Kael's income tax payable by self assessment for 2014/15.

A   £478
B   £7,583
C   £658
D   £7,403   LO 3i

6   In addition to his salary of £9,000, Nibal received the following income in 2014/15:

	£
Tips from customers	250
Interest received on a NISA investment	44
Income tax repayment interest	60

His net income for the year is

A   £9,000
B   £9,250
C   £9,310
D   £9,354   LO 3a

---

7   Paloma, a single woman, was born on 10 May 1947. Her net income for 2014/15 is £27,100.

Select which of the following represents her personal allowance for 2014/15.

A   £10,000
B   £10,400
C   £10,450
D   £10,500   LO 3b

---

8   On 20 May 2014 Charlie, aged 71 married Sarah, aged 80. In 2014/15 Charlie and Sarah had net income of £15,000 and £12,000 respectively.

Select which of the following represents the married couple's allowance as a tax reducer which will be claimed by Charlie for 2014/15.

A   £817
B   £748
C   £680
D   £408   LO 3b

---

9   Perry received income from various sources during 2014/15.

Select which **two** of the following are exempt from income tax.

A   £100 of National Savings & Investments Direct Saver Account interest
B   £80 of National Savings Certificate interest
C   £40 of interest received on a loan to his friend George
D   £56 of dividends received from a shareholding in X plc
E   £40 of dividends received on Y plc shares held in a stocks and shares NISA   LO 3a

---

10   Glenn has employment income of £38,790 assessable in 2014/15. During 2014/15 Glenn also received £270 of dividend income.

What is Glenn's total income tax liability for 2014/15? £ [   ]

Enter a whole number WITHOUT the £ sign   LO 3i

---

11   During 2014/15 Leonard had earnings of £29,351 from his employer. His only other sources of income were a dividend received of £540 and bank interest received of £368. He also paid £351 as a Gift Aid donation to a registered charity.

Select which of the following represents Leonard's taxable income for 2014/15.

A   £30,411
B   £20,259
C   £20,411
D   £19,351   LO 3i

---

12 In 2014/15 Mabel had taxable income of £39,000, all of which represented savings income received gross. She paid £1,056 as a Gift Aid donation to the NSPCC (a registered charity).

Mabel's income tax liability for 2014/15 is £ [   ]

Enter a whole number WITHOUT the £ sign   LO 3i

---

13 During 2014/15 Jacob gave £2,000 to a registered charity. His only income is an annual salary of £50,000.

Identify how Jacob obtains tax relief for his gift.

He receives basic rate tax relief

A   At source by deduction from his salary under payroll giving
B   At source by paying net of basic rate income tax
C   By extending the basic rate band

He receives higher rate tax relief

D   At source by deduction from his salary under payroll giving
E   At source by paying net of basic rate income tax
F   By extending the basic rate band   LO 3i

---

14 Gabriella is self-employed and has trading profits assessable in 2014/15 of £37,145. During 2014/15 she also received the following income:

Building society interest	£480
Premium bond winnings	£250
Dividend income	£720

What is Gabriella's taxable income for 2014/15? £ [   ]

Enter a whole number WITHOUT the £ sign   LO 3a/3i

---

15 Puneet was born on 15 June 1945. His only source of income in 2014/15 is a salary of £27,300.

His personal allowance for 2014/15 is

A   £10,500
B   £10,350
C   £10,200
D   £10,000   LO 3b

---

16 Pierre was born on 10 June 1933. His net income for 2014/15 is £28,040.

His personal allowance for 2014/15 is

A   £10,500
B   £10,000
C   £10,140
D   £10,660   LO 3b

---

17 Margaret is self-employed and has trading profits assessable in 2014/15 of £41,535. During 2014/15 Margaret also received £360 of dividend income.

How much of Margaret's dividend income is subject to tax at 32.5% in 2014/15?

A   £400
B   £360
C   £70
D   £30   LO 3i

18   Maalik is employed by Artichoke Ltd and has employment income in 2014/15 of £30,000, and no other sources of income. On 1 December 2014 Maalik paid £420 to a charity under the Gift Aid provisions. In 2014/15 the Gift Aid payment will

    A   increase Maalik's income tax liability
    B   decrease Maalik's income tax liability
    C   have no impact on Maalik's income tax liability
    D   generate a refund of income tax payable to Maalik   LO 3i

---

19   Bussola has trading profits assessable in 2014/15 of £10,810. During 2014/15 she also received net savings income of £29,280.

Bussola's income tax liability for 2014/15 is £ [   ]

Enter a whole number WITHOUT the £ sign   LO 3i

---

20   Chloe is self-employed and has trading profits assessable in 2014/15 of £22,600. During 2014/15 she also received the following income.

Interest from a NISA	£205
Interest from a NS&I investment account	£190
Dividend income	£360

What is Chloe's net income for 2014/15? £ [   ]

Enter a whole number WITHOUT the £ sign   LO 3a

---

21   Manav has a salary of £27,335 per annum. During 2014/15 he also received the following income.

Income tax repayment interest	£190
Rental income from an investment property	£480

What is Manav's income tax liability for 2014/15? £ [   ]

Enter a whole number WITHOUT the £ sign   LO 3a/3i

---

22   Select which **two** of the following items are treated as 'non-taxable income' for income tax purposes.

    A   Income tax repayment interest
    B   Interest paid on a loan between two friends
    C   National Lottery winnings
    D   Pension income
    E   Tips given to staff by customers   LO 3a

---

23   Frederick works as an employee of Wood Ltd. Frederick's gross salary for 2014/15 was £25,815. During 2014/15 Frederick paid £3,100 in income tax via PAYE.

What is Fredericks's taxable income for 2014/15? £ [   ]

Enter a whole number WITHOUT the £ sign   LO 3i

---

24   Frederick works as an employee of Wood Ltd. Frederick's gross salary for 2014/15 was £25,815. During 2014/15 Frederick paid £3,100 in income tax via PAYE.

What is Frederick's income tax payable under self assessment for 2014/15? £ [   ]

Enter a whole number WITHOUT the £ sign   LO 3i

---

25 Sidney and Bertha were married in February 2007. Sidney is now aged 67 and Bertha is now aged 81. For 2014/15 Sidney has net income of £6,788 and Bertha has net income of £13,456.

Select the option which correctly identifies Sidney's married couple's allowance for 2014/15.

A   Nil – Allocated to Bertha
B   £10,000
C   £8,165
D   £3,140   LO 3b

26 Darcy, aged 29, is self employed and has trading profits assessable in 2014/15 of £198,000.

What is Darcy's personal allowance for 2014/15? £ [   ]

Enter a whole number WITHOUT the £ sign   LO 3b

27 Dave, aged 42, has earnings from employment in 2014/15 of £133,000. He also received bank interest of £22,080 and dividends of £13,500 during 2014/15.

Select which one of the following represents Dave's income tax liability for 2014/15?

A   £59,522
B   £65,147
C   £60,976
D   £64,022   LO 3i

28 Josephine, aged 50, is self employed and has trading profits assessable in 2014/15 of £125,000. During 2014/15 she received dividends of £32,400.

What is Josephine's taxable income for 2014/15? £ [   ]

Enter a whole number WITHOUT the £ sign   LO 3i

1   Emily was born in 1975 and is an employee of Door Ltd with a gross annual salary of £26,000. In addition Emily has taxable benefits worth £2,708. Emily underpaid her tax for 2013/14 by £246. Emily has agreed with HMRC that this underpayment will be collected via her PAYE code for 2014/15.

Select which of the following correctly identifies Emily's PAYE code for 2014/15.

A   606L
B   704L
C   729L
D   1000L   LO 2b

2   Mustafa was born in 1945 and is an employee of Window Ltd with a gross annual salary of £17,000. Mustafa underpaid his tax for 2013/14 by £740. Mustafa has agreed with HMRC that this underpayment will be collected via his PAYE code for 2014/15.

Select which of the following correctly identifies Mustafa's PAYE code for 2014/15.

A   680P
B   865P
C   976P
D   1050P   LO 2b

3   Parminder is 25 and an employee of Sales Ltd with a gross annual salary of £50,000. Parminder also has taxable benefits worth £16,050 for 2014/15.

What is Parminder's PAYE code for 2014/15?

PAYE code   [   ]

Enter a whole number with the appropriate prefix or suffix letter. Do not differentiate between positive or negative numbers.   LO 2b

4   James is 40 years old and earns £60,000 a year. He is entitled to a basic personal allowance. His employer provides him with a company car with a taxable benefit of £11,275.

James' PAYE code for 2014/15 is

A   K126
B   K127
C   K128
D   127L   LO 2b

5   Jacob is 25 years old and earns £15,000 a year. His employer provides him with taxable benefits of £3,060.

Jacob's PAYE code for 2014/15 is [   ] L   LO 2b

6   Dana was born in 1978 and has total income of £50,000 each year. She has underpaid tax of £1,032 in 2013/14 which is recovered through her PAYE code in 2014/15.

Dana's PAYE code for 2014/15 is

A   484L
B   742L
C   896L
D   1000L

LO 2b

7   Harry is an employee of Table Ltd earning a salary of £30,000 per annum. Harry has been provided with a company car for a number of years. The car had a list price of £25,000 and CO_2 emissions of 182g/km. Table Ltd paid for all running expenses of the car including diesel fuel for private use.

The taxable benefits assessable on Harry in 2014/15 are £ ☐

Enter a whole number WITHOUT the £ sign

LO 3c

8   Newburgh Ltd has agreed to provide each of its employees, all of whom earn more than £8,500 per annum and are basic rate taxpayers, with a mobile telephone for the whole of 2014/15. The company will pay £420 per year to hire the telephone inclusive of all calls made by the employees. Newburgh Ltd will also provide its employees with vouchers worth £70 per week for 48 weeks per year for use with an approved child carer.

The additional employment income for each of the company's employees in 2014/15 as a result of the provision of the two benefits is £ ☐

Enter a whole number WITHOUT the £ sign

LO 3c

9   In 2014/15 Jacob was provided with various benefits by his employer Bony Ltd, a manufacturer of televisions, in addition to his salary of £50,000 per annum.

Identify the amount chargeable as employment income for each benefit.

Private health insurance, costing Bony Ltd £800. The same insurance would have cost Jacob £1,100.

A   £800
B   £1,100

A television out of stock which cost £200 to manufacture but would cost Bony Ltd £800 to buy in from another supplier.

C   £200
D   £800

A car parking space at a car park near to the office which cost Bony Ltd £500 in 2014/15.

E   £0
F   £500

LO 3c

10 John works for Ernley Ltd earning a salary of £18,000 per annum. On 1 May 2014 Ernley Ltd provided John with a new company van which had a list price of £6,700 and CO_2 emissions of 116g/km. John uses the vehicle for all business and private purposes. John pays for all of his private fuel.

What is John's taxable benefit for the van in 2014/15?

A   £983
B   £1,072
C   £2,833
D   £3,090

LO 3c

11 James who earns £6,000 per annum is given a bonus in the form of a washing machine by his employer. It cost his employer £700, although it normally retails at £900. James decided that he did not want the washing machine and sold it for £250 to a second hand shop.

Select which of the following is the additional employment income that James will have relating to the washing machine.

A   £0
B   £250
C   £700
D   £900   LO 3c

12 Kyl Ltd has agreed to provide each of its employees with a bicycle costing £850 for use at home and for travelling to work. The bicycles will remain the property of Kyl Ltd. The company will also provide its employees with vouchers worth £25 per week for 44 weeks per year for use with an approved child carer. All of Kyl Ltd's employees earn more than £8,500 per annum and are basic rate or higher rate taxpayers.

How much additional employment income will each of the company's employees have in a full year as a result of the provision of the two benefits?

A   £0
B   £170
C   £1,100
D   £1,270   LO 3c

13 Blanche Ltd purchased a flat in Leeds in 2009 for £310,000. The company's finance director moved into the flat on 1 April 2014 and lived there throughout 2014/15. The market value of the flat on 1 April 2014 was £375,000. The company installed a new kitchen in May 2010 at a cost of £17,000 and double glazing in June 2014 at a cost of £16,000.

The 'cost' of the flat for the purpose of computing the additional yearly rental benefit for 2014/15 is £ [   ]

Enter a whole number WITHOUT the £ sign   LO 3c

14 Amy began working for Samuel Ltd on 6 July 2014. On that day she received a company car with a list price of £20,000 and CO_2 emissions of 172g/km. Samuel Ltd paid for all running expenses of the car including petrol, for Amy's private use.

The taxable benefit assessable on Amy in 2014/15 is £ [   ]

Enter a whole number WITHOUT the £ sign   LO 3c

15 Ping has worked for Brakes Ltd for many years. From 1 July 2014 he had use of a company car with a list price of £15,000 and CO_2 emissions of 187g/km. Brakes Ltd paid for all running expenses of the car except diesel fuel.

The car benefit assessable on Ping in 2014/15 is

A   £3,375
B   £3,713
C   £4,500
D   £4,950   LO 3c

16 Pirro was first provided with a computer by his employer in October 2010 when it was purchased for £2,800. He still has use of the computer for both private and business purposes during 2014/15, although his employers have retained ownership. His private usage of the computer is estimated as 10% of total usage.

The benefit assessable on Pirro in respect of the computer is £ [   ]

Enter a whole number WITHOUT the £ sign   LO 3c

17 Identify whether the following statements are correct or incorrect.

Pippin is provided with a van with CO_2 emissions of 190g/km by his employer Joker Ltd. Joker Ltd pays for all petrol for the van.

Pippin has an assessable fuel benefit based on the CO_2 emissions.

A   Correct
B   Incorrect

Piers makes a nominal contribution towards the fuel cost on his company car of £10 per month. This accounts for about 95% of his private use.

Piers is able to reduce his fuel benefit by £120 pa.

C   Correct
D   Incorrect   LO 3c

18 Monet Ltd purchased a flat in London in 1997 for £280,000. On 1 March 2008, when the flat had a market value of £565,000, Mustafa joined the company and began to live in the flat. The annual gross rateable value of the flat is £8,675.

The taxable benefit of the flat in 2014/15 is £ [   ]

Use an official rate of interest of 3.25%.

Enter a whole number WITHOUT the £ sign   LO 3c

19 Gerrard works for Frame Ltd. He has use of a staff canteen which is available to all employees. The meals in the canteen cost him £1.50 per day although the cost of providing the meals equates to £2.50 per day. He uses the canteen 200 days each year. He was also reimbursed overnight expenses totalling £30 when he worked away from home in Edinburgh for four nights.

How much additional employment income will Gerrard have as a result of the provision of the two benefits?

A   £230
B   £210
C   £30
D   £10   LO 3c

20 Jacob receives a monthly salary of £3,000 and an annual bonus payable on 30 April each year although the bonus actually relates to the previous year ended 31 March. His recent bonuses have been as follows:

Relate to	Date paid	Amount
Year ended 31 March 2014	30 April 2014	£16,500
Year ended 31 March 2015	30 April 2015	£13,400

Which of the following correctly identifies Jacob's employment income assessment for 2014/15?

A   £52,500
B   £49,400
C   £16,500
D   £13,400   LO 3c

---

21 Select whether the following statement is true or false.

Employees in excluded employment are taxed on benefits which can be converted into cash. The assessable amount is the marginal cost to the employer.

A   True
B   False

Select whether the following statement is true or false.

Employees in excluded employment are sometimes called 'P9D' employees.

C   True
D   False   LO 3c

---

22 Emily is provided with a company flat as a benefit of her job in addition to her annual salary of £66,000. Emily's employer rents the flat at an annual cost of £15,000. The annual rateable value of the flat is £8,900. Emily makes a contribution to the rent of £7,000 per annum.

Select which of the following correctly identifies the taxable benefit.

A   £15,000
B   £8,900
C   £8,000
D   £1,900   LO 3c

---

23 Your manager has made the following statements about what qualifies as job related living accommodation.

1   The accommodation is provided for the better performance of an employee's duties and it is customary to be so provided.

2   The accommodation is provided for security reasons.

3   The accommodation enables the employee to work longer hours by reducing time spent commuting.

4   Accommodation provided to directors owning more than 5% of the company is never job related.

Select which one of the following options identifies which of these statements is/are true.

A   All of them
B   1 and 2 only
C   1, 2 and 3 only
D   1, 2 and 4 only   LO 3c

24 Sally is provided with accommodation which originally cost her employer £45,000 in 1981. In 2006 £15,000 was spent on capital improvements. Sally first occupied the property on 6 April 2014 when its market value was £425,000. The annual rateable value of the property is £18,000. Sally has an annual salary of £49,000.

Select which of the following correctly identifies the taxable benefit of the living accommodation for 2014/15.

A   £18,000
B   £11,375
C   £29,375
D   £60,000

Assume an official rate of interest of 3.25%.   LO 3c

---

25 Sumira moved into a house provided by her employer on 6 August 2014. The house cost £465,000 in January 2010. The annual rateable value of the property is £21,000. Sumira's annual salary is £26,000.

Select which of the following correctly identifies the value of the taxable benefit for the living accommodation in 2014/15.

A   £12,675
B   £21,000
C   £22,450
D   £33,675

Assume an official rate of interest of 3.25%.   LO 3c

---

26 Lesley first occupied accommodation provided by her employer on 6 January 2015. The property was originally purchased by her employer in 2011 for £325,000. Capital improvements were made to the property in 2012 at a total cost of £45,000. Lesley pays her employer £12,000 per annum in rent. The annual rateable value of the property is £19,000. Lesley's annual salary is £94,000.

Select which of the following correctly identifies the value of the taxable benefit for the living accommodation in 2014/15.

A   £4,147
B   £16,588
C   £3,781
D   £9,588

Assume an official rate of interest of 3.25%.   LO 3c

---

27 Gertrude has been provided with a petrol company car by her employer since 6 April 2014 in addition to her annual salary of £14,500. The car has CO_2 emissions of 110g/km and a list price of £10,000. Gertrude is also provided with petrol for business and private use. She repays 5p per mile for the private fuel although current petrol prices equate to 15p per mile. Gertrude estimates her private mileage at 5,000 miles for 2014/15.

Select which of the following correctly identifies the taxable benefit for the car and fuel for 2014/15.

A   £4,755
B   £4,505
C   £2,000
D   £1,500   LO 3c

28 Wilma has been provided with a diesel company car for a number of years with CO_2 emissions of 90g/km. It had an original list price of £33,000 although the company bought it second hand for £24,000. Wilma pays her employer £50 per month towards the private use of her car. Wilma has an annual salary of £48,650.

Select which of the following correctly identifies the taxable benefit for the car for 2014/15.

A   £4,620
B   £4,020
C   £3,030
D   £2,760   LO 3c

29 Fred is provided with a two-year-old van by his employer. In addition to home to work journeys, Fred uses the van extensively at weekends. The van has a list price of £8,950 and CO_2 emissions of 111g/km. Fred's employer pays for all his private petrol. Fred's annual salary is £12,455.

Select which of the following correctly identifies the taxable benefit for 2014/15.

A   £4,598
B   £3,671
C   £3,090
D   £1,343   LO 3c

30 Jasper has an annual salary of £4,000 and has received the following benefits during 2014/15:

- Use of a three-year-old company van. Jasper uses the van most of the time as he does not own a car; and

- Gift of video equipment with a market value of £50 which cost £400 six weeks ago.

Select which of the following correctly identifies Jasper's taxable benefits for 2014/15.

A   £3,490
B   £3,140
C   £400
D   £50   LO 3c

31 Robert has an annual salary of £56,000 and has received the following benefits during 2014/15:

- Childcare vouchers of £45 per week or £2,340 per year; and
- Meal vouchers of £5 per day for 240 days of the year.

Robert has been receiving these benefits since 2009.

Select which of the following correctly identifies Robert's taxable benefits for 2014/15.

A   £2,084
B   £3,540
C   £1,200
D   £884   LO 3c

32 Alexandra works for an airline. She has an annual salary of £66,000 and has received the following benefits during 2014/15:

- Gifts of jewellery from a customer worth £200; and

- Provision of free flights when there are spare seats available on the plane. The market value of the flights taken during the year is £4,550.

Select which of the following correctly identifies Alexandra's taxable benefits for 2014/15.

A   £4,750
B   £4,550
C   £200
D   £0   LO 3c

33 Hettie has worked for the same employer (a manufacturing company) for 30 years. She has an annual salary of £12,000 and has received the following benefits during 2014/15.

- Long service award of an original oil painting worth £1,400; and

- Free bus pass worth £455 to enable Hettie to travel from home to work on a public bus service which the employer subsidises.

Select which of the following correctly identifies Hettie's taxable benefits for 2014/15.

A   £1,855
B   £1,400
C   £455
D   £0

LO 3c

34 Sunil is employed as a hairdresser by Hairy Monsters. He is paid £30,000 per annum and provided with a number of benefits.

Select whether the following benefits are taxable or exempt from income tax.

Employer contributions to occupational pension scheme

A   Taxable
B   Exempt

Childcare vouchers for use with an approved provider worth £40 per week

C   Taxable
D   Exempt

Living accommodation

E   Taxable
F   Exempt

LO 3c

35 Charlie commenced work as an employee of House Medical Corporation on 1 July 2014. Charlie earns £35,000 per annum. On 1 July 2014 Charlie was also provided with a company car which runs on diesel with a list price of £18,000 and CO_2 emissions of 160g/km. Charlie pays for all his private fuel.

In calculating Charlie's total employment income for 2014/15, the amount which will be included for the car benefit is £ ☐

Enter a whole number WITHOUT the £ sign

LO 3c

36 Freddie's employer provides him with a diesel company car with a list price of £16,000 on 6 April 2014. The car has CO_2 emissions of 65g/km.

Select which one of the following options correctly identifies Freddie's car benefit for 2014/15.

A   £1,600
B   £800
C   £1,280
D   £2,080

LO 3c

1   Select which **two** of the following statements indicate that a trade is being carried on.

   A   Amy has just sold a house that she bought three months ago. She has spent £40,000 to make the property more attractive to potential purchasers. Amy has not lived in this house.

   B   Ben has sold some shares that he has owned for ten years for substantially more than the original cost.

   C   Caitlin, a student, is experiencing cash flow problems and has had to sell a car that she bought three months ago.

   D   Dante has an interest in vintage cars. He has just sold a car that he has been renovating for the last six months. This is the seventh renovated car that he has sold in the last two years.

LO 3d

2   Select which **two** of the following are not badges of trade.

   A   The number of transactions

   B   Provision of own equipment

   C   Profit seeking motive

   D   Changes to the asset

   E   Correction of own work

LO 3d

3   Paul Sarbanes is a self-employed garage proprietor in Leeds. On 22 December 2014 he made the following gifts.

Identify whether each gift is allowable or disallowable when calculating Paul's tax adjusted trading profit.

A case of wine costing £48 to a customer. Each bottle had the name of the garage on the label.

   A   Allowable

   B   Disallowable

Four bottles of spirits costing £90 to an employee.

   C   Allowable

   D   Disallowable

Cash bonus of £60 to each of his three junior employees.

   E   Allowable

   F   Disallowable

LO 3e

4   Manuel leased a car (CO_2 emissions 123g/km) for use in his business. Manuel took out the lease on 1 May 2014. The hire charges were £5,000 in his year ended 30 September 2014. Manuel used the car, which had a retail price when new of £30,000, 80% of the time for business.

The hire charge allowable as a deduction against trading profits is £ ⬚

Enter a whole number WITHOUT the £ sign

LO 3e

5   Niamh's accounts for the year ended 30 September 2014 showed legal and professional fees of £8,000.

Select which **two** of the following costs are not allowable in calculating her tax adjusted trading profit.

A   Fees incurred in the recovery of a trade bad debt
B   Legal fees of a successful appeal against a tax assessment
C   Renewal of a ten-year lease on business premises
D   Fees for preparation of the annual accounts
E   Cost of taking out a new five-year lease on business premises   LO 3e

6   The following sentences have been included in a draft letter to a client who is about to start a new business.

Identify whether each statement is correct or incorrect.

Expenditure shown in the profit and loss account is not always allowable for tax purposes. Disallowable expenditure must be added back when computing the taxable trading profits.

A   Correct

B   Incorrect

The building that you are acquiring is dilapidated and requires repair work. You are not able to use the building until this work has been completed. The additional expenditure incurred on this repair work is allowable when computing taxable trading profits.

C   Correct

D   Incorrect   LO 3e

7   Noah is a wine merchant with a year ended 31 March 2015. Identify which **two** of the following are allowable expenses in calculating Noah's taxable trading profits.

A   A gift of a £10 bottle of wine to each of 200 potential new customers as a marketing method to entice them to buy more wine in the future

B   Gifts to his two employees of a wine hamper costing him £60 for each employee

C   Legal costs relating to the acquisition of a 25-year lease on new business premises

D   Donation to a national charity   LO 3e

8   Flynn has been a sole trader for many years. His profit and loss account to the 31 January 2015 includes the following items of expenditure.

Identify which **two** are fully allowable in calculating Flynn's taxable trading profits.

A   Costs of registering a patent for trade use

B   Payment of a parking fine incurred by Flynn while travelling on business

C   Payment of £12,000 to his wife Freya for working as one of his shop assistants. The other assistants earn £8,000 per annum for working similar hours

D   The legal costs for renewing the ten-year lease on his shop premises   LO 3e

9   William Pitt is a self-employed tax adviser in Coventry. In the year ended 31 March 2015 he made the following gifts. All of the recipients are registered charities.

(i)   To the renovation fund for Coventry Cathedral (a local charity)
(ii) To the World Wide Fund for Nature (a national charity) via the Gift Aid Scheme
(iii) To the National Trust (a national charity)

Select which of the following options shows which gifts(s) is/are allowable when computing William's trading profits assessment?

A   All of them
B   (iii) only
C   (i) and (ii) only
D   (i) only   LO 3e

10 Penha has a hobby restoring antique furniture. He has just sold a restored antique table that he has owned for several years. He sold ten items of restored furniture in 2014/15.

Select which **two** of the following badges indicate that Penha is carrying on a trade in relation to this disposal.

A   The number of transactions
B   Interval of time between purchase and sale
C   Changes to the asset
D   Correction of own work   LO 3d

11 Imogen is a sole trader and her accounts show £7,700 on repairs and maintenance during the year to 30 September 2014.

Repair to a newly acquired second hand machine to make it useable	£2,400
Repairs to the roof of the office damaged in a storm	£3,800
Redecorating the office	£1,500

How much should be added back to the accounting profit for tax purposes?

A   £2,400
B   £3,900
C   £5,300
D   £7,700   LO 3e

12 Marion has been trading as a shopkeeper for many years. Her latest accounts show the following expenditure.

	£
Annual salary to Peter, Marion's husband, who has worked in the shop on Saturdays (Note: Saturday workers are paid £3,000 per annum)	14,000
Total motor expenses relating to Marion's car (business usage agreed at 60%)	800

Select which of the following represents the amount to be added back to the accounting profit.

A   £14,800
B   £14,320
C   £11,800
D   £11,320   LO 3e

13 Barry's business has the following bad debt account for the year to 31 March 2015.

	£		£
Written off:		Balance brought forward	
Trade debts	3,600	– specific debts	4,600
Loan to former employee	500		
		Debt recovered – loan to	
		former employee	
Balance carried forward		previously written off	200
– specific debts	5,200	Profit & loss account	4,500
	9,300		9,300

Select which of the following is the adjustment required.

A   Add back £300
B   Add back £500
C   Add back £900
D   Deduct £300

LO 3e

14 Peter's accounts for the year ended 31 March 2015 include the following items within travel and entertaining:

	£
Flight to Aberdeen to visit a potential new customer. Peter delayed his return journey to spend a long weekend with friends at a ski resort close to Aberdeen.	250
Hospitality box at Aintree racecourse to entertain customers	4,050
Staff annual dinner dance (£200 per head)	3,800

Select which of the following is the amount to be added back in the accounts.

A   £4,050
B   £4,300
C   £7,850
D   £8,100

LO 3e

15 Bruce and Kieran are in partnership selling and repairing computers. Their accounts include the following expenditure.

Speeding fines for Bruce	£490
Gift of computer software to a local school	£1,200
Subscriptions to a computer trade magazine	£150

What are the total disallowable expenses?

A   £490
B   £640
C   £1,350
D   £1,690

LO 3e

16   Michelle's accounts include the following items.

Penalty for the late submission of VAT return	£270
Legal fees for the renewal of a short lease	£750
Employer's pension costs accrued (amount actually paid is £2,300)	£2,500

What are Michelle's total disallowable expenses?

A   £1,020
B   £950
C   £470
D   £270   LO 3e

17   Barbara is a sole trader and leases a car with a retail price of £16,000 and CO_2 emissions of 152g/km. The car is used 100% for business purposes by Barbara. The annual leasing charge is £3,800. She took out the lease on 1 May 2014.

Select which of the following is the adjustment that Barbara needs to make in her accounts for tax purposes for the year ended 31 January 2015.

A   £3,230 added back
B   £428 added back
C   £570 added back
D   £3,372 added back   LO 3e

18   Paola is a sole trader. She has deducted the two items listed below in arriving at her draft tax adjusted profits of £46,223 for the year ended 28 February 2015.

Select whether an adjustment to profits should be made for each of the following items in order to determine Paola's final tax-adjusted trading profits.

A restaurant bill for £432 for a staff party attended by Paola and all three employees

A   Adjust
B   Do not adjust

Staff costs of £3,298 relating to work undertaken preparing the accounts for the business by Paola's husband

C   Adjust
D   Do not adjust   LO 3e

19   Andy is a sole trader and a higher rate tax payer. His accounting profit for the year ended 31 March 2015 includes a deduction of £938, which is the amount of a donation made to a local hospital under the Gift Aid scheme on 1 February 2015.

Select whether the following statements are true or false relating to this donation.

An amount of £938 must be added back to the accounting profit to arrive at the adjusted trading profit

A   True
B   False

The basic rate band must be extended by £938 to correctly calculate Andy's tax liability

C   True
D   False   LO 3e/3i

20 Donna owns a shoe shop that she has run as a sole trader for many years. In the year ended 31 December 2014 she took shoes for herself from the shop which had cost £220. The shoes retailed at a total of £450. No adjustment has been made in the accounts relating to the shoes.

The amount by which accounting profits need to be increased to arrive at trading profits, in relation to the shoes is £ [   ]

Enter a whole number WITHOUT the £ sign   LO 3e

21 Sam has a landscape gardening business, which he runs as a sole trader. In the year ended 31 March 2015 the salaries and wages account of the business is as follows.

	£
Salaries (including £27,000 for Sam)	55,000
Class 1 secondary contributions	2,766
Class 2 contributions	143
Pension contributions for Sam (all paid during the accounting period)	2,700
	60,609

The amount to be added back in calculating tax adjusted trading profit is

A   £27,000
B   £27,143
C   £29,700
D   £29,843   LO 3e

22 Paul and Jill set up in partnership on 1 April 2014. The partnership accounts for the year ended 31 March 2015 include legal and professional fees as follows.

	£
Accountancy fees	2,000
Legal fees on the preparation of the partnership agreement	800
Legal fees relating to the acquisition of a new 10 year lease on the office premises	1,500
Legal fees for recovery of trade debts	400
	4,700

The amount to be added back in calculating the tax adjusted profits is £ [   ]

Enter a whole number WITHOUT the £ sign   LO 3e

23 Jem is a VAT registered sole trader. He has deducted the following two items listed below in calculating his draft tax adjusted profits of £92,421 for the year ended 31 December 2014.

Select whether an adjustment to profits should be made for each of the following items in order to determine Jem's final tax-adjusted trading profits.

A bill from a hotel for £480 (including VAT of £80) for a meal that Jem had with a major UK customer

A   Add back £480
B   Add back £400
C   Do not adjust

A bill from a hotel for £5,000 (excluding VAT) for the annual staff party costing £200 per head

D   Add back £5,000
E   Do not adjust   LO 3e

24 Sam is a sole trader with an accounting profit of £42,674 for the year ended 31 March 2015. The following two items are included in the accounts in arriving at the accounting profit.

Select what adjustment, if any, needs to be made to arrive at the tax adjusted trading profit.

Bank interest received of £280 on the business bank account.

A   Deduct £280
B   Deduct £350
C   Do not adjust

Profit of £490 on disposal of a machine

D   Add £490
E   Deduct £490
F   Do not adjust   LO 3e

25 James is a sole trader drawing up accounts to 31 January. The motor expenses account for the year ended 31 January 2015 is as follows.

	£
Costs relating to James' car (70% business use)	2,000
Costs relating to the sale manager's car (80% business use)	1,800
Hire purchase interest payable on James' car	400
	4,200

Select which of the following is the amount to be added back when calculating the tax adjusted trading profit.

A   £600
B   £720
C   £960
D   £1,080   LO 3e

26 Caroline is a sole trader and identified the following amounts which have not been included in her accounts.

Select how each item should be treated in the adjustment to profits working in order to determine Caroline's tax adjusted trading profit.

Caroline has personally paid for her home telephone bills which include calls of £1,000 of which 30% relates to business

A   Increase trading profits by £300
B   Reduce trading profits by £300
C   Do not include in calculating tax adjusted trading profits

Caroline made a £200 donation to a local hospice, this was not paid under the Gift Aid scheme

D   Increase trading profits by £200
E   Reduce trading profits by £200
F   Do not include in calculating tax adjusted trading profits   LO 3e

27 Soria deducted the following amounts in arriving at her taxable trading profits of £65,329 for the year ended 31 March 2015.

Select whether an adjustment to profits should be made for each of the following items in order to determine Soria's final tax adjusted trading profit.

£10,000 of salary to her husband who works as a bookkeeper for her business

A   Adjust
B   Do not adjust

Irrecoverable VAT of £3,500 on a company car purchased for an employee

C   Adjust
D   Do not adjust   LO 3e

28 Tariq charged the following items in arriving at his net trading profit for the year to 31 March 2015:

	£
Amount written off debtors relating to a client who is in liquidation	4,800
Interest on late payment of income tax	1,234

Select which one of the following options correctly identifies the amount which should be disallowed when calculating Tariq's tax adjusted trading profits for the year.

A   £0
B   £1,234
C   £4,800
D   £6,034   LO 3e

1   Nina began trading on 1 May 2014 and prepared accounts for the year ended 30 April 2015. On 1 August 2014 she purchased a photocopier for £2,300 and a car with emissions of 128g/km for £2,300. The photocopier and the car are used for business purposes for 90% of the time.

The maximum capital allowances that Nina will receive in respect of the purchase of the photocopier in the year ended 30 April 2015 are

A   £2,300
B   £2,070
C   £373

The maximum capital allowances that Nina will receive in respect of the purchase of the car in the year ended 30 April 2015 are

D   £2,300
E   £414
F   £373   LO 3e

2   Aasia began trading on 1 June 2014 and prepared accounts for the period ended 31 March 2015. On 1 December 2014 she purchased a photocopier for £3,000 and a car with emissions of 125g/km for £3,000. The photocopier and the car are only used for business purposes.

The maximum capital allowances that Aasia will receive in respect of the purchase of the photocopier in the period ended 31 March 2015 are

A   £3,000
B   £540
C   £450

The maximum capital allowances that Aasia will receive in respect of the purchase of the car in the period ended 31 March 2015 are

D   £3,000
E   £540
F   £450   LO 3e

3   Leona began trading on 1 October 2014, preparing her first accounts to 31 January 2015. On 1 December 2014 she purchased a computer for £5,000 and a car with emissions of 125g/km for £13,200. Both assets are only used for business purposes.

The maximum capital allowances available on the computer in the period to 31 January 2015 are

A   £5,000
B   £1,667
C   £300

The maximum capital allowances available on the car in the period to 31 January 2015 are

D   £13,200
E   £2,376
F   £792   LO 3e

4   Barbara began trading on 6 April 2014. Her tax adjusted trading profit for the year ended 5 April 2015 is £17,430 before the deduction of capital allowances. On 1 December 2014 Barbara purchased a van for £13,200. The van is used by her 80% of the time for business purposes and has CO_2 emissions of 120g/km.

Select which of the following is the maximum capital allowance claim available to Barbara for the year ended 5 April 2015.

A   £1,901
B   £2,376
C   £10,560
D   £13,200

LO 3e

5   The following sentences have been included in a draft letter to a client who is about to start a new business.

Identify whether each statement is correct or incorrect.

Expenditure is only allowable for the purposes of computing trading profits if it has been incurred wholly, exclusively and necessarily for the purposes of the trade

A   Correct
B   Incorrect

Capital expenditure is not allowable in computing trading profits but will always result in capital allowances

C   Correct
D   Incorrect

LO 3e

6   Select which **two** of the following statements are correct.

A   Expenditure is only allowable for the purposes of computing trading profits if it has been incurred wholly, exclusively and necessarily for the purposes of the trade.

B   Capital expenditure is not allowable in computing trading profits but will sometimes result in capital allowances.

C   Expenditure is only allowable for the purposes of computing trading profits if it has been incurred wholly and exclusively for the purposes of the trade.

D   The charge to the profit and loss account in respect of an increase to a bad debt provision is never allowable for the purposes of computing trading profits.

E   Capital expenditure is not allowable in computing trading profits but will always result in capital allowances.

LO 3e

7   Murphy began trading on 6 April 2014 and drew up his first accounts to 5 April 2015.

He made the following purchases of assets.

		£
1 July 2014	Machinery	514,000
1 September 2014	Motor car	16,000

Murphy used the motor car only for business purposes. It is a qualifying low emission car.

Murphy's maximum capital allowances for the period ended 5 April 2015 are £ [   ]

Enter a whole number WITHOUT the £ sign

LO 3e

8   Murray and Nuri have been trading in partnership for many years with a year end of 31 March.

The tax written down values of their assets at 1 April 2014 were:

		£
Murray's car – purchased 1 April 2010	Private use 40%, emissions 125g/km	17,000
Nuri's car – purchased 1 July 2010	Private use 30%, emissions 135g/km	8,000

Nuri's car was sold on 1 July 2014 for £6,000. Nuri intends to lease a car from this date.

The partnership's maximum capital allowances for the year ended 31 March 2015 are £ [   ]

Enter a whole number WITHOUT the £ sign   LO 3e

9   Jack has been trading for many years making up accounts to 31 March.

The only asset in the business for the purpose of capital allowances is a car bought in 2011 with CO_2 emissions of 120g/km, which Jack uses 75% for business purposes. The tax written down value of the car at 1 April 2014 was £15,000.

On 1 September 2014 Jack sold the car for £10,200.

Select which one of the following are the maximum capital allowances available to Jack for the year ended 31 March 2015?

A   £2,025
B   £2,700
C   £3,600
D   £4,800   LO 3e

10   Mary, who runs a business, purchased the following assets in the year ended 31 May 2015.

		£
12 February 2015	Computer	10,000
20 March 2015	Car – emissions of 84g/km and used wholly for business purposes	8,000
1 May 2015	Office furniture	2,000

What are the maximum capital allowances available to Mary?

Capital allowances   £ [   ]

Enter a whole number WITHOUT the £ sign   LO 3e

11   Ming-Na commenced to trade as a sole trader on 1 September 2014 preparing her first set of accounts for the nine months ended 31 May 2015.

On 1 November 2014 Ming-Na purchased a car with emissions of 130g/km for £18,000. She uses this 60% for business purposes.

Calculate the maximum capital allowances available for the car for the nine months ended 31 May 2015.

Capital allowances   £ [   ]

Enter a whole number WITHOUT the £ sign   LO 3e

12 Harry is a sole trader. In the year ended 31 March 2015 he sold a car for £14,500 which had a tax written down value brought forward at 1 April 2014 of £17,000. Harry used the car 70% for business purposes.

Select which one of the following represents the balancing adjustment on disposal of the car in the year ended 31 March 2015.

A   Balancing allowance of £2,500
B   Balancing charge of £2,500
C   Balancing allowance of £1,750
D   Balancing charge of £1,750

LO 3e

13 Jack is a sole trader with accounts prepared to 31 May each year. In the year ended 31 May 2015 Jack purchased a car with emissions of 127g/km for £18,000. The car is driven by one of his employees who uses it 20% of the time for private purposes.

The maximum amount of capital allowances that can be claimed in the year ended 31 May 2015 relating to this car is £ ⬚

Enter a whole number WITHOUT the £ sign

LO 3e

14 Pauline began trading as a sole trader on 1 October 2014, preparing her first set of accounts for the six months ended 31 March 2015. On the 1 January 2015 she purchased a new car with emissions of 125g/km for £16,000 (it is used only for business purposes).

Select which one of the following options correctly identifies the maximum amount of capital allowances Pauline may claim for the six months ended 31 March 2015.

A   £640
B   £1,440
C   £2,880
D   £16,000

LO 3e

15 Alex is a sole trader. He has plant and machinery with a tax written down value of £560 on 1 July 2014. During the nine-month accounting period to 31 March 2015, he purchased a computer for £8,000.

Select which one of the following options correctly identifies the maximum amount of capital allowances available to Alex for the nine months ended 31 March 2015.

A   £8,560
B   £8,076
C   £1,541
D   £1,156

LO 3e

16 Matthew is a sole trader and has prepared accounts for the year to 31 December 2014. At 1 January 2014 the business only owned one asset, a machine. The £12,000 cost of the machine had been put in the main pool when it was acquired several years ago. The balance on the main pool at 1 January 2014 was £2,300. The machine was sold on 30 June 2014 for £400. Matthew's business is continuing, but he now leases all machinery.

The maximum capital allowances that can be claimed by Matthew for the year ended 31 December 2014 are £ ⬚

Enter a whole number WITHOUT the £ sign

LO 3e

17 Max is a sole trader with a year ended 30 September 2014. The balance on the main pool at 1 October 2013 was £25,400. The only capital transaction was the disposal of a machine on 10 August 2014 for £4,300. The machine had cost £3,900 in April 2012.

The maximum capital allowances that can be claimed by Max for the year ended 30 September 2014 are   £ ⌷

Enter a whole number WITHOUT the £ sign   LO 3e

18 Peter runs a business and prepared accounts for the six months to 31 March 2015. The tax written down value of the main pool at 1 October 2014 was £24,000. During the period of account, the following transaction took place.

		£
20 December 2014 Purchased new low emission car		9,000

Calculate the maximum amount of capital allowances Peter may claim for the six months ended 31 March 2015.

A   £5,940
B   £9,000
C   £11,160
D   £13,320   LO 3e

19 Charlie, a sole trader, prepared accounts for the five months ended 31 March 2015. On 23 November 2014 he purchased a machine for £260,000.

Select which one of the following represents the maximum capital allowances that can be claimed in respect of this machine for the period ended 31 March 2015.

A   £260,000
B   £212,208
C   £217,633
D   £208,333   LO 3e

20 Select which one of the following assets will **not** be in a single asset pool for capital allowance purposes.

A   Computer costing £10,000 with 30% private use by the owner of the business

B   Car with emissions of 125g/km costing £14,000 on 10 June 2014 with 20% private use by one of the employees

C   Car with emissions of 125g/km costing £13,000 on 1 January 2015 with 35% private use by the owner of the business

D   Delivery van costing £15,000 with 10% private use by the owner of the business   LO 3e

21 Jamie is a sole trader with a year ended 31 January 2015. The balance on the main pool at 1 February 2014 was £31,000. The only capital transaction was the disposal of a machine on 10 August 2014 for £5,300. The machine had originally cost £9,900.

The maximum capital allowances that can be claimed by Jamie for the year ended 31 January 2015 are £ ⌷

Enter a whole number WITHOUT the £ sign   LO 3e

22 Janice is a sole trader with a year ended 5 April 2015. On 1 May 2014 Janice bought a machine costing £520,000.

The maximum capital allowances that can be claimed by Janice on the machine for the year ended 5 April 2015 are £ ▢

Enter a whole number WITHOUT the £ sign

LO 3e

Chapter 7: Trading profits – basis of assessment

1 Rafael, Saeed and Tadeo have been in partnership for many years. The partnership agreement allocates a salary of £10,000 per annum to Saeed and all partners receive 5% per annum on their capital invested. The balance of any profits is shared equally.

During the year ended 30 June 2014 Rafael's capital account had a balance of £60,000, Saeed's balance was £24,000 and Tadeo's was £38,000. The partnership made trading profits of £125,000 in the year ended 30 June 2014.

The trading profits assessable on Rafael in 2014/15 are £ [   ]

Enter a whole number WITHOUT the £ sign   LO 3f

2 Townshend ceased trading on 30 November 2014. The recent tax adjusted trading profits of his business are as follows.

	£
Year ended 30 April 2013	38,000
Year ended 30 April 2014	34,000
Period ended 30 November 2014	23,000

Townshend has unrelieved overlap profits of £7,000.

What is Townshend's trading profit assessment for 2013/14?

A £38,000
B £34,000
C £34,334

What is Townshend's trading profit assessment for 2014/15?

D £16,000
E £50,000
F £57,000   LO 3h

3 Jabir and Kadin began trading in partnership on 1 September 2014, sharing profits equally. The partnership agreement allocates an annual salary to Jabir of £8,000. For the year ended 31 August 2015 the partnership had a tax adjusted trading profit of £105,000.

Select which option correctly shows the partners' assessable trading profits for 2014/15.

A   Jabir £56,500   Kadin £48,500
B   Jabir £32,958   Kadin £28,292
C   Jabir £60,500   Kadin £52,500
D   Jabir £35,292   Kadin £30,625   LO 3f/3g

4   James commenced in business on 1 October 2014.

Select which one of the following will result in no overlap profits.

A   First accounts are year ended 30 September 2015 with future accounts to 30 September
B   First accounts are 6 months ended 5 April 2015 with future accounts to 5 April
C   First accounts are 3 months ended 31 December 2014 with future accounts to 31 December
D   First accounts are 4 months ended 31 January 2015 with future accounts to 31 January   LO 3g

5   Val, Cliff and Frank have been in partnership for many years preparing accounts to 30 September each year. The partnership agreement indicates that all partners receive 5% per annum on their capital invested. The balance of any remaining profits is shared equally.

During the year ended 30 September 2014 Val's capital account had a balance of £50,000, Cliff's balance was £30,000 and Frank's was £40,000. The partnership made trading profits of £150,000 in the year ended 30 September 2014.

The trading profits assessable on Cliff in 2014/15 are £ [   ]

Enter a whole number WITHOUT the £ sign   LO 3f

6   Tom and Dick have been trading in partnership for many years, sharing profits in the ratio 2:1. The partnership agreement allocates an annual salary to Tom of £10,000. The partnership had the following results.

Year ended 31 October 2014   £120,000
Year ended 31 October 2015   £150,000

Select which one option correctly shows the partners' assessable trading profits for 2014/15.

A   Tom £80,000   Dick £40,000
B   Tom £83,333   Dick £36,667
C   Tom £100,000   Dick £50,000
D   Tom £103,333   Dick £46,667   LO 3f

7   Raanan ceased trading on 31 December 2014. The recent tax adjusted trading profits of his business are as follows.

	£
Year ended 31 January 2013	40,000
Year ended 31 January 2014	25,000
Period ended 31 December 2014	15,000

Raanan has unrelieved overlap profits of £8,000.

Raanan's trading profit assessment for 2014/15 is £ [   ]

Enter a whole number WITHOUT the £ sign   LO 3h

8   John started trading on 1 January 2013, but his business quickly ran into cash flow problems and he ceased to trade on 28 February 2015. The accounts for the year ended 31 December 2013 showed taxable trading profits of £6,000, and those for the period from 1 January 2014 to 28 February 2015 showed taxable trading profits of £2,800.

Select which of the following represents John's taxable trading profit for 2014/15?

A   £2,800
B   £2,400
C   £1,300
D   £900   LO 3g/3h

9   Trevor's business has unrelieved overlap profits brought forward of £4,000. He ceased trading on 30 April 2014. The recent tax adjusted trading profits of his business are as follows.

	£
Year ended 30 September 2012	24,000
Year ended 30 September 2013	30,000
Period ended 30 April 2014	25,000

What are Trevor's taxable trading profits for 2014/15?

A   £55,000
B   £51,000
C   £25,000
D   £21,000   LO 3h

10 Obed commenced trading on 1 July 2014, preparing his first accounts to 30 June 2015. The adjusted trading profits for the year ended 30 June 2015 were £24,000.

Select which of the following amounts is Obed's assessable trading profit for 2014/15.

A   £6,000
B   £18,000
C   £20,000
D   £24,000   LO 3g

11 Nadeem commenced trading on 1 July 2014, preparing his first accounts to 30 June 2015. The adjusted trading profits for the year ended 30 June 2015 were £24,000.

Select which of the following amounts is Nadeem's overlap profit on commencement of trade.

A   £6,000
B   £18,000
C   £20,000
D   £24,000   LO 3g

12 Raeleen commenced trading on 1 January 2014, preparing her first accounts to 30 June 2014 and she will prepare them to every following June. The adjusted trading profits are as follows.

	£
6 months ended 30 June 2014	10,000
Year ended 30 June 2015 (estimated)	25,000

Select which **two** of the following statements are correct.

A   Taxable trading profits for 2014/15 are £25,000
B   Taxable trading profits for 2013/14 are £5,000
C   Taxable trading profits for 2013/14 are £22,500
D   Taxable trading profits for 2014/15 are £22,500   LO 3g

13 Ben commenced trading on 1 January 2014, preparing his first accounts to 30 June 2015. The adjusted trading profits for the period ended 30 June 2015 were £42,000.

Select which of the following statements is correct.

A   £28,000 is taxable in 2014/15, representing the period 6 April 2014 to 5 April 2015
B   £28,000 is taxable in 2014/15, representing the year ended 30 June 2015
C   £7,000 is taxable in 2014/15, representing the period 1 January 2014 to 5 April 2014
D   £42,000 is taxable in 2014/15, representing the period to 30 June 2015   LO 3g

14 Ray commenced trading on 1 July 2014, preparing his first accounts to 31 December 2014. The adjusted trading profits for the first two periods were

	£
6 m/e 31 December 2014	60,000
12 m/e 31 December 2015 (estimate)	100,000

The taxable trading profit for 2014/15 is £ [   ]

Enter a whole number WITHOUT the £ sign   LO 3g

---

15 Ray commenced trading on 1 July 2014, preparing his first accounts to 31 December 2014. The adjusted trading profits for the first two periods were

	£
6 m/e 31 December 2014	60,000
12 m/e 31 December 2015 (estimate)	100,000

Ray's overlap profits are £ [   ]

Enter a whole number WITHOUT the £ sign   LO 3g

---

16 Amber and Betty have been trading in partnership for many years, sharing profits in the ratio 2:1. On 1 July 2014 they changed the arrangement so that a salary of £20,000 pa is allocated to Amber and the remaining profits are shared equally. The partnership made adjusted trading profits of £240,000 in its year ended 31 December 2014.

Select which option correctly shows the partners' assessable trading profits for 2014/15.

A   Amber £120,000   Betty £120,000
B   Amber £140,000   Betty £100,000
C   Amber £135,000   Betty £95,000
D   Amber £145,000   Betty £95,000   LO 3f

---

17 Aubrey and Elaine have been in partnership for many years. Both partners are allocated interest of 5% per annum on their capital invested. The balance of any profits is shared equally.

During the year ended 30 September 2014 Aubrey's capital account had a balance of £50,000, Elaine's was £20,000. The partnership made trading profits of £100,000 in the year ended 30 September 2014.

The trading profits assessable on Aubrey in 2014/15 are £ [   ]

Enter a whole number WITHOUT the £ sign   LO 3f

---

18 David and Doreen started in partnership together on 1 July 2014 sharing profits in the ratio 2:1. The partnership taxable trading profit for the year ended 30 June 2015 is £120,000.

Select which of the following is the amount of trading profits taxable on Doreen in 2014/15.

A   £80,000
B   £60,000
C   £40,000
D   £30,000   LO 3f/3g

19   Florian ceased trading on 30 September 2014. The recent tax adjusted trading profits of his
      business are as follows:

	£
Year ended 31 January 2013	28,500
Year ended 31 January 2014	21,200
Period ended 30 September 2014	17,430

      Florian has unrelieved overlap profits of £2,610.

      Florian's taxable trading profit for 2014/15 is   £ [   ]

      Enter a whole number WITHOUT the £ sign   LO 3h

20   Imogen began trading on 1 August 2014 and her first accounts to 31 May 2015 showed an
      adjusted trading profit before deduction of capital allowances of £65,000.

      She made the following purchases of assets.

		£
1 August 2014	Office equipment	10,000
1 September 2014	Motor car with emissions of 124g/km	16,000
1 April 2015	Office shelving	500

      Imogen used the motor car only for business purposes.

      Imogen's assessable trading profits for 2014/15 are   £ [   ]

      Enter a whole number WITHOUT the £ sign   LO 3e/3g

21   Jennifer Cavendish began trading on 1 November 2014. Her tax adjusted trading profit for the
      period ended 30 June 2015 is £23,520 before deduction of capital allowances. Jennifer purchased a
      car on 1 November 2014 for £7,680. The car has emissions of 122g/km and is used for business
      purposes only.

      Jennifer's trading profit assessment for 2014/15 is   £ [   ]

      Enter a whole number WITHOUT the £ sign   LO 3e/3g

22   Leroy and Annabelle have been in partnership for many years. The partnership agreement allocates
      partners' interest at 5% pa on capital invested. The balance of any profits is shared in the ratio 2:3.

      On 31 December 2014 Leroy's capital account had a balance of £35,000 and Annabelle's balance
      was £23,000. For the year ended 31 December 2014 the partnership had a tax adjusted trading
      profit of £98,500.

      Select the option which correctly shows Leroy's assessable trading profits for 2014/15.

      A   £41,150
      B   £39,990
      C   £39,400
      D   £38,240   LO 3f

23 Parminder commenced to trade on 1 January 2014 making up her first set of accounts to 28 February 2015. Her tax adjusted profits after capital allowances are as follows.

Period ended 28 February 2015   £53,208
Year ending 28 February 2016   £31,740 (estimate)

Select which of the following options correctly identifies Parminder's trading profits for 2014/15.

A   £53,208
B   £45,607
C   £44,451
D   £31,740

LO 3g

24 Na is a sole trader and uses the cash basis. During the year to 30 April 2015 she had total receipts of £63,000. This included a receipt of £3,000 from the sale of a car.

Her payments for the year to 30 April 2015 totalled £27,000. This included interest paid of £600. At 30 April 2015 Na had prepaid rent on business premises of £1,000 relating to May and June 2015.

What is Na's taxable trading profit for the year ended 30 April 2015? Ignore capital allowances.

A   £37,000
B   £33,000
C   £36,100
D   £33,100

LO 3e

25 Oscar started to trade as a sole trader on 1 July 2014 and has elected to use the cash basis for tax purposes. He has tax adjusted total receipts for the ten months ended 30 April 2015 of £58,000. He has tax adjusted total payments for the period of £31,000.

Select the option which correctly shows Oscar's assessable trading profits for 2014/15.

A   £24,300
B   £27,000
C   £52,200
D   £58,000

LO 3e

Remember that when calculating NIC you should round mathematically at each step of the computation.

1   Sho has his own business and has adjusted trading profits for the year of £5,100 (accounts profits of £5,900). He also has a part-time job earning £9,500 each year.

Select which **two** of the following types of national insurance contributions Sho must pay in relation to 2014/15.

A   Class 1 primary
B   Class 1 secondary
C   Class 2
D   Class 4   LO 1d

2   Robert, aged 59, is a director of Wagner Ltd, a company in which he owns 50% of the shares. He takes £50,000 a year out of the company, £20,000 as a salary, the balance as dividends.

The company employs George, aged 63, as Robert's personal assistant. His annual salary is £15,000.

The company makes a profit of £80,000 before tax and before accounting for the amounts paid to Robert.

Identify which of the following statements concerning NICs is/are correct.

Wagner Ltd will pay Class 4 NICs on the profits of £80,000.

A   Correct
B   Incorrect

George will pay Class 1 primary NICs on his earnings of £15,000.

C   Correct
D   Incorrect

Wagner Ltd will pay Class 1 secondary NICs on total employee remuneration of £65,000, before deducting the employment allowance.

E   Correct
F   Incorrect   LO 1d/3j

3   Steven has the following details for 2014/15.

	£
Adjusted trading profits before capital allowances	15,000
Capital allowances	2,500

Steven's Class 4 national insurance contributions for 2014/15 are £ [   ]

Enter a whole number WITHOUT the £ sign   LO 3j

4   James has been trading for many years. His adjusted trading profits for the last two years have been as follows.

	£
Year ended 5 April 2014	41,000
Year ended 5 April 2015	45,000

What are his Class 4 national insurance contributions for 2014/15?

A   £3,052
B   £3,115
C   £3,334
D   £2,974   LO 3j

---

5   Abe has been trading for many years. His adjusted trading profits for 2014/15 are £20,000.

His total national insurance contributions for 2014/15 are £ [   ]

Enter a whole number WITHOUT the £ sign   LO 3j

---

6   During 2014/15 Ball Ltd pays Lena, one of its 25 employees, a salary of £38,862. The company provides her with a car that has a cash equivalent benefit of £5,000, and a car parking space near to the office which costs the company £500 pa.

The Class 1 secondary contributions payable by Ball Ltd in 2014/15 in respect of Lena are
£ [   ]

Ignore the employment allowance.

Enter a whole number WITHOUT the £ sign   LO 3j

---

7   During 2014/15 Ball Ltd pays Lena a salary of £38,862 and provides her with a car that has a cash equivalent benefit of £5,000, and a car parking space near to the office which costs the company £500pa.

The Class 1A contributions payable by Ball Ltd in 2014/15 in respect of Lena are £ [   ]

Enter a whole number WITHOUT the £ sign   LO 3c/3j

---

8   Boris, aged 68, has a part time job working for Jinx Ltd, earning £7,700 each year.

Identify whether the following statements are correct.

Boris will have Class 1 primary contributions deducted from his wages

A   Correct
B   Incorrect

Jinx Ltd must pay Class 1 secondary contributions in relation to Boris's earnings

C   Correct
D   Incorrect   LO 1d

9   Cobalt Ltd made a trading profit of £50,000 in its year ended 31 March 2015.

The company employs only Bain, aged 62, on an annual salary of £35,610.

The total national insurance liability of the company for 2014/15 is £ ⬚

Enter a whole number WITHOUT the £ sign   LO 3j

10 During 2014/15 Bat Ltd pays Barry a salary of £45,000 and provides him with benefits totalling £3,000.

What are the national insurance contributions payable by Bat Ltd in 2014/15 in respect of Barry?

Ignore the employment allowance.

A   £6,624
B   £5,112
C   £5,526
D   £4,805   LO 3j

11 Sam is employed full time as a bricklayer working for Homes Ltd. One weekend he agrees to build a garden wall for his neighbour in return for a lump sum payment of £2,000. Sam has never undertaken paid work outside his employment before.

Indicate whether Sam will be liable to pay each of the following taxes on this £2,000 lump sum payment.

Capital gains tax

A   Yes
B   No

Income tax

C   Yes
D   No

National insurance

E   Yes
F   No   LO 1d

12 Adam is about to commence trading in partnership with Zak. Which of the following statements is true?

A   Adam must register to pay Class 2 national insurance within six months of the end of the tax year.

B   Adam and Zak must each register to pay Class 2 NICs by the date the first partnership return is due.

C   Adam must register to pay Class 2 NICs as soon as possible after commencing to trade.

D   The partnership must register to pay Class 2 NICs as soon as possible after commencing to trade.

LO 1c

13 During 2014/15 Trim Ltd pays Belinda a monthly salary of £3,300. In addition, Trim Ltd paid Belinda a bonus of £4,000 in December 2014.

The total national insurance liability of Belinda for 2014/15 is £ [   ]

Enter a whole number WITHOUT the £ sign   LO 3j

Chapter 9: Capital gains tax – individuals

1   The Quack partnership has recently disposed of an office building. The office building was owned jointly by all the partners. The office building was sold to a property developer.

Select which option correctly identifies the person(s) liable to pay any capital gains tax due on the disposal of the office building.

A   Partnership
B   Partners jointly
C   Property developer
D   Partners individually   LO 1d/ 4a

2   Jamie entered into a contract with Annabelle to purchase a house. Contracts were exchanged on 15 March 2015. The contracts were completed and legal title therefore passed on 15 April 2015. Once contracts had been exchanged neither party could withdraw. Payment was not made until 17 April 2015 and Jamie did not physically move into the house until 18 April 2015.

Select which of the following options correctly identifies the date on which Annabelle will be treated as having disposed of the house for capital gains tax purposes.

A   15 March 2015
B   15 April 2015
C   17 April 2015
D   18 April 2015   LO 1d

3   Select which of the following statements about capital gains is true.

A   Assets which are inherited are treated as being acquired by the donee at the price originally paid by the donor

B   Wasting chattels bought and sold for more than £6,000 are chargeable to CGT

C   Stamp duty land tax paid on the purchase of land may be deducted as part of cost on a subsequent disposal of the land

D   Where an asset is not sold at arm's length, the proceeds are deemed to equal cost so that no chargeable gain arises   LO 4a/4b

4   Katie sold an antique vase which she had purchased in January 1989 for £13,000. She sold it for £5,600 in March 2015 and paid auctioneer's fees of £800 for its sale. Select which of the following options correctly identifies Katie's allowable loss on sale.

A   £(7,800)
B   £(8,200)
C   £(7,400)
D   £(7,000)   LO 4b

5   Freddy made two disposals during 2014/15.

      For each of the two disposals select how the resulting gains should be treated to determine
      Freddy's total chargeable gains for 2014/15.

      Gain of £4,500 on the disposal of a caravan.

      A   Chargeable gain

      B   Exempt

      Gain of £1,000 on the sale of a sculpture. The sculpture originally cost £4,000.

      C   Chargeable gain

      D   Exempt   LO 4a

---

6   Thomas purchased an antique chair in February 2001 for £2,500. He sold it in May 2014 for
      £11,150. He paid £560 as commission to the agent who sold the chair for him.

      Select which of the following options correctly identifies the chargeable gain on the disposal of the
      chair.

      A   £8,650
      B   £8,583
      C   £7,650
      D   £8,090   LO 4b

---

7   David has net income for 2014/15 of £48,995. David has also made taxable gains of £33,422 for
      2014/15.

      Select how each of the following items will affect the calculation of David's capital gains tax liability
      for 2014/15, if at all.

      His unused annual exempt amount from 2013/14

      A   Reduces capital gains tax payable

      B   Increases capital gains tax payable

      C   No effect

      Becoming a higher-rate taxpayer for the first time
      D   Reduces capital gains tax payable

      E   Increases capital gains tax payable

      F   No effect   LO 4c

---

8   The Goose partnership has recently disposed of a chargeable asset. The chargeable asset was
      owned jointly by all the partners.

      Select which option correctly identifies the person(s) liable to pay any capital gains tax due on the
      disposal of the chargeable asset.

      A   Partners individually
      B   No capital gains tax is due
      C   Partnership
      D   Partners jointly   LO 1d

---

9   In December 1997 Jasmine purchased a house for £176,000. Jasmine has always rented out the house to tenants. In December 2000 Jasmine installed a new bathroom at a cost of £6,400. In December 2014 Jasmine sold the house for £642,000. Jasmine also paid stamp duty land tax at 1% of the purchase price when she bought the house.

What is the chargeable gain on disposal of the house?

Chargeable gain   £ [   ]

Enter a whole number WITHOUT the £ sign   LO 4b

---

10 Jed purchased a rare painting in August 2004 for £3,200. He sold it in August 2014 for £14,150. He paid £142 as commission to the agent who sold the painting for him.

Select which of the following options correctly identifies the chargeable gain on the disposal of the painting.

A   £10,808
B   £10,950
C   £13,583
D   £13,347   LO 4a/4b

---

11 Select which **two** of the following items are exempt assets for capital gains tax purposes.

A   £15,000 of shares in an unquoted trading company
B   A diamond necklace purchased for £1,000 and now worth £17,000
C   A rare collection of snakes worth £320,000
D   £10,000 of National Savings Certificates   LO 4a

---

12 Select which of the following disposals is a chargeable disposal for capital gains tax purposes.

A   Bequest of a house in the will of a mother to her daughter
B   Gift to a friend of £12,000 in National Savings Certificates
C   Gift to a friend of a painting worth £1,000,000
D   Gift of a painting to a charity when the painting was worth £300,000   LO 4a

---

13 Justin entered into a contract with Matthew to purchase a rare art collection. Contracts were exchanged on 1 March 2015 subject to a final valuation being done. The valuation took place on 1 April 2015. Legal title finally passed on 5 April 2015. Payment was not made until 7 April 2015.

Select which of the following options correctly identifies the date on which Matthew will be treated as having disposed of the art collection for capital gains tax purposes.

A   1 March 2015
B   1 April 2015
C   5 April 2015
D   7 April 2015   LO 1d

14 Select which of the following statements about capital gains is true.

A CGT is chargeable on individuals, partnerships and companies

B Stamp duty land tax paid on the purchase of land may not be deducted as part of cost on a subsequent disposal of the land

C Assets which are inherited are treated as being acquired by the donee at their value at the time of the donor's death

D Where an asset is sold by an individual, indexation allowance will decrease the chargeable gain

LO 1d/4b

15 Harry made two disposals during 2014/15.

For each of the disposals select how the resulting gains should be treated to determine Harry's total chargeable gains for 2014/15.

Gain of £2,500 on the disposal of a car.

A Chargeable gain

B Exempt

Gain of £3,000 on the sale of a greyhound, which originally cost £4,000.

C Chargeable gain

D Exempt

LO 4a

16 Identify which of the following does not pay tax on its chargeable gains.

A NSPCC, a registered charity
B WFT plc, a quoted company
C George and Bert, who are in partnership together
D Bert, in his own right as an individual

LO 4a

17 Identify which of the following is **not** a chargeable disposal made by Gordon.

A The sale of a building used by Gordon's business, to a third party
B The gift of shares to Gordon's son
C The loss of a painting valued at £50,000 during a fire at Gordon's house
D The gift of an antique table valued at £40,000 to Gordon's daughter on his death

LO 4a

18 Peter purchased a holiday home in July 2003. The holiday home cost £100,000 and he paid solicitor's fees of £2,500 relating to the purchase.

During 2004 he spent £2,800 on a garage for the holiday home and £580 on repairs to the plaster work when there was a flood. Peter anticipates selling the house within the next few months.

The total allowable expenditure on the disposal of the holiday home will be

A £100,000
B £102,500
C £105,300
D £105,880

LO 4b

19 Identify which **two** of the following are not exempt wasting chattels for the purposes of capital gains tax.

A   Office furniture, purchased for use only in Jack's business office on which he claims capital allowances

B   A racehorse purchased as an investment by Max

C   Goodwill of a computer manufacturing business with an expected life of 20 years

D   A caravan, purchased by David for use on family holidays   LO 4a

20 Identify whether each of the following disposals will be chargeable or exempt.

Javier sold a painting at auction and received £5,900 after deducting auctioneers fees of £310. The painting had originally cost him £3,500

A   Chargeable

B   Exempt

Savion received £2,600 for some shares that he sold after deducting £150 of fees. The shares originally cost him £800

C   Chargeable

D   Exempt   LO 4a

21 Lourdes bought an antique brooch for £4,000 in October 2003. In January 2015, she sold it on the internet and received £6,200 after deduction of £100 fees. Lourdes' chargeable gain is

A   £333
B   £500
C   £2,200
D   £2,300   LO 4b

22 In February 2004 Nuria purchased a painting for £6,700. She sold it at auction for £4,600, after deducting £200 of auctioneer's fees, in October 2014.

The allowable loss on disposal is

A   £(2,300)
B   £(2,100)
C   £(700)
D   £(900)   LO 4b

23 Identify which one of the following may result in a chargeable gain.

A   A gift of a painting worth £250,000 to a local art gallery
B   A sale of shares in Beagle plc by the RSPCA, a registered charity
C   A gift of antique jewellery worth £25,000 by Robert, to his daughter as a wedding gift
D   James sold gilt edged securities valued at £40,000 to his friend Arthur for £27,000   LO 4a

24 On which **two** of the following disposals must a chargeable gain/allowable loss be calculated?

    A   A sale of shares in Check plc by Cristiano. The shares were held in an ISA

    B   Torey cashed in his National Savings Certificates in order to raise money for his wedding

    C   Townsend lost an antique ring valued at £8,000, and received a cheque from the insurance company for that sum

    D   Toshi sold a painting for £5,000. It was given to him several years ago when his grandfather died. At that time it was worth £6,400

LO 4a

25 Fraser sold a diamond brooch at auction in June 2014, and received £7,900 after deduction of auctioneer's fees of £300. The brooch had cost him £6,100 in July 2000. Since then he had spent £250 in August 2001 having it cleaned and repaired. In September 2004 he paid £400 to have additional diamonds and rubies added to the brooch.

Fraser's chargeable gain on disposal of the brooch is £ [   ]

Enter a whole number WITHOUT the £ sign

LO 4b

26 Identify whether each of the following disposals will be chargeable or exempt.

Erwin sold a painting at auction and received £6,100 after deducting auctioneer's fees of £200. The painting had originally cost him £3,500.

    A   Chargeable

    B   Exempt

Eryk received £5,900 for jewellery that he sold. The jewellery originally cost him £5,900 plus auctioneer's fees of £200.

    C   Chargeable

    D   Exempt

LO 4a

27 Ervin bought an antique vase for £4,000 in October 2005. In January 2015, he sold it for £6,300. Assuming the annual exempt amount is used up by other disposals, Ervin's taxable gain on the vase is

    A   £0
    B   £500
    C   £2,000
    D   £2,300

LO 4b

28 In February 2004 Ebeneezer purchased a painting for £5,900. He sold it at auction for £5,600 after deducting £150 of auctioneer's fees in October 2014.

The allowable loss on disposal is

    A   £0
    B   £(300)
    C   £(50)
    D   £(150)

LO 4b

29　Select which **two** of the following assets are exempt assets for capital gains tax purposes.

　　A　An antique diamond necklace worth £3,000 (cost £2,500)

　　B　A small hotel

　　C　An oil painting worth £12,000 (cost £9,000)

　　D　Fixed plant and machinery sold at a profit

　　E　Shares held in a NISA　　　　　　　　　　　　　　　　　　　　　　　　　LO 4a

30　On 1 December 2014 David sold his holiday cottage for £200,000. He had bought the cottage in July 1999. The table below shows David's expenditure on the cottage prior to its sale.

　　Select which **three** of these costs will be deducted in calculating David's chargeable gain.

　　A　Legal fees on purchase　　　　　　　　　　　　£800

　　B　Purchase price　　　　　　　　　　　　　£110,000

　　C　Redecoration costs　　　　　　　　　　　　£2,100

　　D　Cost of building a garage　　　　　　　　　£7,500

　　E　Replacement of a few roof tiles after a storm　　£150　　　　　　　　　　LO 4b

31　Martha has recently made two disposals. For each of the two disposals select how the resulting gains or losses should be treated in the computation of Martha's taxable gains.

　　Gain of £3,600 on the sale of goodwill in her ice cream van business

　　A　Chargeable gain

　　B　Exempt

　　Loss of £2,000 on the sale of a diamond necklace which had cost £4,000

　　C　Allowable capital loss

　　D　Exempt　　　　　　　　　　　　　　　　　　　　　　　　　　　　　　LO 4a

32　Joshua has draft taxable gains of £30,500 for 2014/15 including the two items below. Select how Joshua's draft taxable gains will be affected by the correct treatment of each item.

　　A gain of £4,200 on the sale of his ten-year old racehorse

　　A　No effect

　　B　Increase

　　C　Decrease

　　Auctioneer's fees of £500 have been deducted in arriving at the £13,400 gain on sale of an antique sculpture at an auction

　　D　No effect

　　E　Increase

　　F　Decrease　　　　　　　　　　　　　　　　　　　　　　　　　　　　　LO 4c

33 In March 1989, Matthew purchased an office for £642,000. Matthew sold the office in March 2015 for £1,250,100, incurring £120,000 estate agents' fees on the sale.

Matthew made no other disposals of chargeable assets during 2014/15. Matthew has taxable income of £27,495 in 2014/15.

Select which option correctly identifies Matthew's capital gains tax liability for 2014/15.

A   £136,231
B   £133,151
C   £169,831
D   £166,751

LO 4c

1 In January 1990, Sink Ltd purchased a property. In December 2001 Sink Ltd built an extension to the property. In September 2014 Sink Ltd sold the property.

Select which option correctly identifies the indexation factor which should be used to calculate the indexation on the extension.

A 1.165
B 0.451
C 0.943
D 0.492

RPIs are as follows:

January 1990 119.5
December 2001 173.4
September 2014 258.7   LO 4b

2 Pineapple plc sold an antique writing desk which had been purchased in January 1996 for £18,000. It was sold for £3,200 in January 2015. The proceeds were received net of selling fees of £400.

Select which of the following options correctly identifies Pineapple plc's allowable loss.

A £(12,000)
B £(12,400)
C £(15,200)
D £(25,486)

RPIs are as follows:

January 1996 150.2
January 2015 259.4   LO 4b

3 Shower plc has made two disposals in its year ended 31 August 2015.

For each of the two disposals select how the resulting gains should be treated in the calculation of Shower plc's chargeable gains.

Gain of £24,000 on the disposal of a rare African snake which had not been used in the business.

A Chargeable gain

B Exempt

Gain of £1,100 on the sale of an antique chair. The chair originally cost £5,000.

C Chargeable gain

D Exempt   LO 4a

4   Pasta plc sold one of its warehouses on 1 July 2014 for £2,125,000. The warehouse originally cost £432,000 in February 1986. On disposal Pasta plc paid estate agents fees of £24,969. At acquisition legal fees were £3,000 and stamp duty land tax was £12,960. During its ownership Pasta plc added a canteen to the building at a cost of £48,000.

What is Pasta plc's unindexed gain on this disposal?

Unindexed gain   £ [   ]

Enter a whole number WITHOUT the £ sign   LO 4b

---

5   Pumpkin Ltd purchased a plot of land in August 1991 for £60,000. The company sold it in November 2014, incurring £750 for advertising.

Identify which of the following is the indexation allowance relating to the disposal.

A   £55,860
B   £56,558
C   £55,839
D   £56,537

RPIs are as follows:

August 1991   134.1
November 2014   258.9   LO 4b

---

6   Party Ltd purchased a building for investment purposes in March 1996 for £150,000. The company sold it in September 2014 for £425,000. The indexation factor to apply to the disposal is 0.708.

The gain in Party Ltd's corporation tax computation for the year ended 31 December 2014 is

A   Nil
B   £275,000
C   £157,800
D   £168,800   LO 4b

---

7   Identify which one of the following statements is correct.

A   For individuals and companies there is an annual exempt amount available to reduce the amount of gains taxable each year

B   Individuals and partnerships will be able to reduce their gains by indexation allowance

C   Capital gains tax is payable by individuals and companies on their taxable gains

D   Individuals will have a chargeable gain on disposal of goodwill from their business   LO 1d/4b

---

8   Tractor Ltd realised a chargeable gain of £16,000 on disposal of a building in January 2015. The only other income of the company in its year ended 31 March 2015 was trade profits of £10,000.

The tax suffered by Tractor Ltd on its chargeable gain is

A   £2,880
B   £1,000
C   £3,200
D   £3,360   LO 4c

9   Lettuce Ltd was incorporated on 11 May 2014. It opened an interest bearing building society account on 1 July 2014 and commenced to trade on 1 January 2015. It will make up its first set of accounts to 30 September 2015 and annually thereafter.

Select which of the following options correctly identifies Lettuce Ltd's first accounting period for corporation tax purposes.

A   11 May 2014 – 31 December 2014
B   1 July 2014 – 31 December 2014
C   1 January 2015 – 30 September 2015
D   1 January 2015 – 31 December 2015   LO 5a

10 Aquarius plc allowed the following amounts in arriving at its draft trade profits of £53,000.

Select how each item should be treated in the adjustment to profits working in order to determine Aquarius plc's final trade profits.

Aquarius plc included £1,090 relating to the profit on disposal of an item of machinery

A   Add back £1,090

B   Deduct £1,090

C   Do not adjust

Aquarius plc included an expense of £21,400 relating to director bonuses and salaries (the directors are also the majority shareholders)

D   Add back £21,400

E   Deduct £21,400

F   Do not adjust   LO 5c

11 Capricorn plc has calculated the following amounts which have yet to be included in its final trade profits.

Select how each item should be treated in the adjustment to profits working in order to determine Capricorn plc's final trade profits.

Capricorn plc has calculated a balancing charge of £500 arising as a result of the disposal of plant

A   Increase trade profits by £500

B   Reduce trade profits by £500

C   Do not include in trade profits

Capricorn plc made a £100 donation to the local children's hospital after one of its employee's children was treated there

D   Increase trade profits by £100

E   Reduce trade profits by £100

F   Do not include in trade profits   LO 5c

12 Sagittarius plc deducted the following amounts in arriving at its draft trade profits of £654,544 for the year ended 31 January 2015.

Select whether an adjustment to profits should be made for each of the following items in order to determine Sagittarius plc's final trade profits for tax purposes.

£599 of legal costs relating to the renewal of a 25-year lease

A   Adjust

B   Do not adjust

Irrecoverable VAT of £3,500 on a company car purchased for an employee

C   Adjust

D   Do not adjust   LO 5c

---

13 Virgo Ltd, a manufacturing company, included £35,000 relating to pension costs in arriving at its draft trade profits for the year ended 31 December 2014. This included a closing accrual of £12,000 with only the balance actually being paid into a registered pension scheme during the year.

Select which of the following options correctly identifies the amount to be added back in order to determine Virgo Ltd's final trade profits.

A   £0
B   £12,000
C   £23,000
D   £35,000   LO 5c

---

14 Pisces Ltd included £26,500 relating to interest costs in arriving at its draft trade profits. £20,000 related to interest payable on a loan used to build a new factory, including a closing accrual of £4,000. The remaining £6,500 related to interest payable on a loan used to purchase shares in a subsidiary.

Select which of the following options correctly identifies the amount of interest costs which is actually allowable against trade profits.

A   £0
B   £16,000
C   £20,000
D   £26,500   LO 5c

---

15 Scorpio plc charged the following items in arriving at its net profit for the year to 31 March 2015:

	£
Amount written off stock to reduce it to net realisable value	4,600
Interest on late payment of corporation tax	16,456

Select which of the following options correctly identifies the amount which should be disallowed when calculating Scorpio plc's trade profits for the year.

A   £0
B   £4,600
C   £16,456
D   £21,056   LO 5c

16 Rome plc charged the following items in arriving at its net profit for the year to 31 March 2015:

	£
Gifts of industrial trade samples to UK customers	950
Gifts to UK customers (one calendar each) – wall calendars bearing company logo costing £46.50 each	4,650

Select which of the following options correctly identifies the amount which should be allowed when calculating Rome plc's trade profits for the year.

A   £0
B   £950
C   £4,650
D   £5,600   LO 5c

17 Paris plc prepared its first set of accounts for the twelve months ended 31 March 2015. On 1 January 2015 it purchased a new car for £14,400 (CO_2 emissions 120g/km).

Select which of the following options correctly identifies the maximum amount of capital allowances Paris plc may claim for the twelve months ended 31 March 2015.

A   £648
B   £2,592
C   £3,600
D   £14,400   LO 5c

18 Copenhagen Ltd prepares accounts to 31 March each year. The tax written down value of the main pool at 1 April 2014 was £13,400. During the year ended 31 March 2015, the following transaction took place:

	£
2 January 2015 Sold car (cost £10,000 in May 2009)	3,500

Calculate the maximum amount of capital allowances Copenhagen Ltd may claim for the year ended 31 March 2015.

Capital allowances   £ [   ]

Enter a whole number WITHOUT the £ sign   LO 5c

19 Select which **two** of the following statements about corporation tax are true.

A   A company with taxable total profits of £1.5m in both the current year and the prior year will pay corporation tax at the main rate.

B   A company with a short accounting period must have profits of at least £300,000 before it will pay corporation tax at more than the small profits rate.

C   A company with five associates will have higher limits for the purposes of corporation tax rates compared to the limits for a group of six companies.

D   The correct marginal relief formula is: fraction × (relevant upper limit – augmented profits) × taxable total profits/augmented profits.   LO 5b/5d

20   Walnut Ltd has no associated companies and taxable total profits of £950,000 for the year ended 31 March 2015. During the year Walnut Ltd received gross exempt dividends from UK companies of £100,000.

Select which of the following options correctly identifies the amount of marginal relief available to Walnut Ltd for the year ended 31 March 2015.

A   £0
B   £1,018
C   £1,244
D   £1,375   LO 5d

21   Peanut plc had taxable total profits of £35,000 for the year ended 31 January 2015. Peanut plc has no associated companies. During this accounting period, Peanut plc received exempt cash dividends of £7,200.

Select which of the following options correctly identifies the amount of corporation tax payable by Peanut plc for the year ended 31 January 2015.

A   £7,467
B   £8,600
C   £8,440
D   £7,000   LO 5d

22   Cashew Ltd drew up accounts for the six month period to 30 June 2015. Cashew Ltd pays interest on its £20,000 9% debenture stock annually on 31 March.

Select which of the following options correctly identifies the amount of interest allowable for tax purposes for the six months ended 30 June 2015.

A   £720
B   £900
C   £1,440
D   £1,800   LO 5c

23   Monkey plc has taxable total profits of £850,000 and a dividend received of £18,000 for the six months ended 31 December 2014. Monkey plc has no associated companies.

Select which of the following options correctly identifies the amount of corporation tax payable for the six months ended 31 December 2014.

A   £170,000
B   £176,961
C   £178,500
D   £182,700   LO 5d

24   Gorilla Ltd commenced trading on 1 April 2014 and purchased a motor car for £8,500 (a low emissions car) for the use of an employee (75% business use, 25% private).

Select which of the following options correctly identifies the maximum amount of capital allowances Gorilla Ltd may claim on the car for the six months ended 30 September 2014.

A   £3,188
B   £4,250
C   £6,375
D   £8,500   LO 5c

25 Giraffe Ltd received exempt cash dividends of £36,000 from its wholly owned UK subsidiary in the year ended 31 May 2015. During the year it also received exempt dividends of £4,500 from a 10% holding in Lion Ltd.

Select which of the following options correctly identifies the amount of franked investment income for Giraffe Ltd for the year ended 31 May 2015.

A   £4,500
B   £5,000
C   £40,500
D   £45,000

LO 5d

26 Select which one of the following statements about corporation tax is true.

A   A company which is centrally managed and controlled in the UK will always be liable to UK corporation tax on its worldwide profits.

B   A company which is incorporated in the UK will only be liable to UK corporation tax on its worldwide profits if it is also centrally managed and controlled in the UK.

C   A company which is incorporated abroad and centrally managed and controlled abroad, will still be liable to UK corporation tax on its worldwide profits.

D   A company which is incorporated abroad will never be liable to UK corporation tax on its worldwide profits.

LO 1d

27 In the year ended 31 July 2015, Cat Ltd has bank interest receivable of £103,000 and interest payable as set out below.

	£
On loan to acquire investment property	14,000
On loan to acquire factory premises	42,000
On loan to acquire shares in a subsidiary company	6,000

Select which of the following options correctly identifies Cat Ltd's assessable non-trading loan relationship credits for the year ended 31 July 2015 and the amount of interest which is deductible in arriving at the company's trade profits?

	Non-trading Loan relationships	Trading deduction
A	£41,000	£0
B	£61,000	£20,000
C	£83,000	£42,000
D	£97,000	£56,000

LO 5c/5d

28 Aubrey Stainton, an individual, owns 100% of the share capital of Budgie Ltd and Goldfish Ltd. Budgie Ltd has taxable total profits of £118,000 for the year ended 31 March 2015. Following the preparation of the company's corporation tax computation, it was realised that no account had been taken of either of the following factors:

(i)   Budgie Ltd paid a dividend of £24,000 on 1 December 2014 to Aubrey.

(ii) Budgie Ltd received an exempt gross dividend of £27,000 on 1 March 2015 from Hamster Ltd. Budgie Ltd owns 5% of the shares in Hamster Ltd.

Select which of the following options correctly identifies which of the above dividends will have an effect on the corporation tax liability of Budgie Ltd?

A   Both of them
B   Neither of them
C   (i) only
D   (ii) only

LO 5d

29 Labrador Ltd has incurred the following legal expenses in its first accounting period.

	£
Preparation of directors' employment contracts (the directors are also the shareholders)	4,600
Issue of share capital	2,000
Acquiring a 30-year lease	3,000

Select which of the following options correctly identifies the amount of legal expense which is disallowed for tax purposes.

A £2,000
B £3,000
C £5,000
D £9,600

LO 5c

30 Collie plc commenced trading on 1 August 2014 and purchased a motor car (CO_2 emissions 123g/km) for £16,800 for the use of a director (25% private use). Collie plc prepared its first accounts for the eight months to 31 March 2015.

Calculate Collie plc's maximum capital allowance available for the car for the eight months ended 31 March 2015.

Maximum capital allowance for the car £ [   ]

Enter a whole number WITHOUT the £ sign

LO 5c

31 Alsatian Ltd has plant and machinery with a tax written down value of £20,000 on 1 September 2014. During the seven month accounting period to 31 March 2015, it purchased a machine for £7,000.

Select which of the following options correctly identifies the maximum amount of capital allowances available to Alsatian Ltd for the seven months ended 31 March 2015.

A £4,860
B £2,835
C £9,100
D £10,600

LO 5c

32 Setter Ltd has forecast the following results for its year ended 31 December 2015.

	£
Trading income	50,000
UK dividends received in cash from 15% holding in Boxer Ltd	18,000
Chargeable gain	7,500
Qualifying donation paid to UNICEF (a registered charity)	(8,000)

Select which of the following options correctly identifies Setter Ltd's augmented profits.

A £67,500
B £49,500
C £77,500
D £69,500

LO 5d

33 Dalmatian Ltd has the following results for the year ended 31 March 2015.

	£
Taxable total profits	1,434,060
Exempt UK dividends received (gross)	5,940

Dalmatian Ltd has no associated companies.

Select which of the following options correctly identifies the amount of marginal relief to which Dalmatian Ltd is entitled for the year ended 31 March 2015.

A   £0
B   £149
C   £164
D   £165   LO 5d

34 Airedale Ltd was incorporated on 11 June 2014. It opened an interest bearing building society account on 1 August 2014 and commenced to trade on 1 February 2015. It makes up its first set of accounts to 30 September 2015 and annually thereafter.

Select which one of the following options correctly identifies Airedale Ltd's first accounting period for corporation tax purposes.

A   1 August 2014 – 31 July 2015
B   11 June 2014 – 31 January 2015
C   1 February 2015 – 30 September 2015
D   1 August 2014 – 31 January 2015   LO 5a

35 Select which **two** of the following statements about corporation tax are true.

A   Exempt gross dividends received from non-associated UK companies are used to determine a company's corporation tax rate.

B   Companies may deduct qualifying donations paid and accrued when calculating taxable total profits.

C   Dividends paid by a company are a valid business expense.

D   Interest paid on a loan to purchase a new factory is a trading expense.

E   Charitable donations made to national charities are allowable against trading income. LO 5c/5d

36 Dachshund plc receives the following gross amounts of exempt dividends during December 2014.

	£
From Doberman Ltd, a wholly owned UK subsidiary	45,000
From Pointer Ltd, Dachshund plc holds 2.5% of the issued share capital	26,000
From Greyhound Ltd, Dachshund plc acquired its entire 50.1% holding on 1 November 2014	34,000

Select which of the following options correctly identifies the amount of dividends which will give rise to franked investment income for the year ended 31 December 2014.

A   £105,000
B   £26,000
C   £79,000
D   £60,000   LO 5d

37 Hovawart plc included the following amounts in arriving at its draft trading income of £666,888 for the year ended 31 May 2015.

Select whether an adjustment to profits should be made for each of the following items in order to determine Hovawart plc's final trading income.

Depreciation of £156,742

A   Adjust

B   Do not adjust

Interest of £1,500 received on a loan to an employee

C   Adjust

D   Do not adjust   LO 5c

38 Russell plc allowed the following amounts in arriving at its draft trading income of £1,555,000.

Select how each item should be treated in the adjustment to profits working in order to determine Russell plc's final trading income.

Russell plc included £4,000 relating to the loss on disposal of an item of machinery

A   Add back £4,000

B   Deduct £4,000

C   Do not adjust

Russell plc included £144,400 relating to redundancy costs (employees received an amount equal to their annual salary)

D   Add back £144,400

E   Deduct £144,400

F   Do not adjust   LO 5c

39 Spitz plc has calculated the following amounts which have yet to be included in its final trading income.

Select how each item should be treated in the adjustment to profits working in order to determine Spitz plc's final trading income.

Spitz plc has calculated a balancing charge of £2,500 arising as a result of a disposal from the main pool

A   Increase trading income by £2,500

B   Reduce trading income by £2,500

C   Do not include in trading income

Spitz plc sponsored three employees for £100 each for taking part in a marathon on behalf of Oxfam (an internationally registered charity)

D   Increase trading income by £300

E   Reduce trading income by £300

F   Do not include in trading income   LO 5c

40 Newfoundland Ltd, a trading company, included £47,300 relating to pension costs in arriving at its draft trading income. In addition, £17,000 being an opening accrual was paid. No closing accrual was required.

Select which of the following options correctly identifies the amount of the adjustment required in order to determine Newfoundland Ltd's final trading income.

A   £17,000
B   £0
C   £64,300
D   £47,300   LO 5c

41 Pug Ltd included £33,400 relating to interest costs in arriving at its draft trading income. £13,000 related to interest payable on a loan used to purchase new machinery. The remaining £20,400 related to interest payable on a loan used to buy an investment.

Select which of the following options correctly identifies the amount of interest costs which is actually allowable against trading income.

A   £0
B   £13,000
C   £33,400
D   £20,400   LO 5c

42 Papillon Ltd has taxable total profits of £350,000 for its three month accounting period to 31 December 2014. Papillon Ltd has franked investment income for the same period of £30,000. Papillon has no associated companies.

Calculate Papillon Ltd's corporation tax liability for the three months ended 31 December 2014.

Papillon Ltd's corporation tax liability £ [   ]

Enter a whole number WITHOUT the £ sign   LO 5d

43 Rottweiler Ltd acquired £1,540,000 of 10% debentures for investment purposes on 1 January 2015. Interest is payable half yearly on 31 December and 30 June each year. Accordingly, Rottweiler Ltd did not actually receive any interest during the year to 28 February 2015.

Select which of the following options correctly identifies the amount of interest taxable in the year ended 28 February 2015.

A   £154,000 as trading income
B   £25,667 as a non-trading loan relationship credit
C   £0
D   £154,000 as a non-trading loan relationship credit
E   £25,667 as trading income   LO 5c/5d

44 Schnauzer plc had taxable total profits of £215,000 for the eight months ended 31 January 2015. Schnauzer plc has no associated companies.

Select which of the following options correctly identifies the amount of corporation tax payable by Schnauzer plc for the eight months ended 31 January 2015.

A   £41,937
B   £45,150
C   £43,187
D   £43,000

LO 5d

45 Corgi plc had taxable total profits for the ten months ended 28 February 2015 of £656,000. Corgi plc also received exempt gross dividends of £13,000 from its 10% holding in Queenie Ltd. Corgi plc has no associated companies.

Select which of the following options correctly identifies the amount of marginal relief available to Corgi plc for the ten months ended 28 February 2015.

A   £1,424
B   £2,037
C   £1,456
D   £0

LO 5d

46 Select which one of the following statements about corporation tax is true.

A   A company with taxable total profits of less than £1.5 million will never pay corporation tax at the main rate.

B   A company with augmented profits of £300,000 will always pay corporation tax at the small profits rate on its taxable total profits.

C   A company with no associated companies and a six month accounting period will pay corporation tax at the main rate only if its augmented profits exceed £1.5 million.

D   A company might pay corporation tax at a higher rate if it receives exempt dividends from UK companies in which it has shareholdings of less than 50%.

LO 5d

47 Whippet plc has taxable total profits of £36,000 for the year ended 31 March 2015. During the year Whippet plc paid dividends of £8,000 to corporate shareholders. Whippet plc has no associated companies.

Select which of the following options correctly identifies Whippet plc's corporation tax liability for the year ended 31 March 2015.

A   £7,560
B   £7,200
C   £8,978
D   £5,600

LO 5d

48 Arabesque Ltd prepared its first set of accounts for the eight months ended 31 October 2014. On 1 May 2014 it purchased a new car for £18,000 (CO_2 emissions of 129g/km).

Select which of the following options correctly identifies the maximum amount of capital allowances Arabesque plc may claim for the eight months ended 31 October 2014.

A   £2,160
B   £3,240
C   £12,000
D   £18,000

LO 5c

49 Pirouette Ltd prepares accounts to 31 March each year. The tax written down value of the main pool at 1 April 2014 was £890. During the period of account, the following transaction took place:

£

31 June 2014   Purchased new delivery van   10,000

Calculate the maximum amount of capital allowances Pirouette Ltd may claim for the year ended 31 March 2015.

Capital allowances   £ [   ]

Enter a whole number WITHOUT the £ sign   LO 5c

---

50 Select which one of the following statements about corporation tax is true.

A   The correct marginal relief formula is always:
     fraction × (£1,500,000 – augmented profits) × taxable total profits/augmented profits.

B   Companies with taxable total profits of £1.5m pay corporation tax at the main rate.

C   A group of five companies will have higher limits for the purposes of corporation tax rates compared to the limits for a company with four associates.

D   A company with a short accounting period must have augmented profits of at least £300,000 before it will pay corporation tax at more than the small profits rate.   LO 5b/5d

---

51 Fouette plc owns 50.2% of the shares in Tutu Ltd which in turn owns 50.1% of the shares in Plie Ltd. Fouette plc also owns 100% of the shares in Pointe SA, a company incorporated and managed and controlled in France. Fouette plc also has a 75% shareholding in a dormant company called Brise plc. All companies, excluding Brise plc are trading companies.

Select which of the following options correctly identifies the number of associated companies for the purposes of calculating the rate of corporation tax.

A   Three
B   Five
C   Two
D   Four   LO 5b

---

52 Rain plc is a trading company with a year end of 31 October. Rain plc purchased 100% of the shares in Thunder Ltd on 1 November 2014. Rain plc has owned 49% of the shares in Cloud Ltd which in turn owns 85% of the shares in Wind Ltd for a number of years.

Select which of the following options correctly identifies the associated companies for the purposes of calculating the correct corporation tax rates for the year ended 31 October 2014.

A   Rain plc, Wind Ltd and Thunder Ltd
B   Cloud Ltd and Wind Ltd
C   Rain plc and Wind Ltd
D   Rain plc, Cloud Ltd, Wind Ltd and Thunder Ltd   LO 5b

53   H Ltd holds 75% of S Ltd. S Ltd in turn holds 65% of S2 Ltd.

Select which of the following statements about these companies is true.

A   Assuming none of the companies has been sold in the current accounting period, there are three associates

B   Assuming all the companies are liable to UK corporation tax, there are three associates

C   H's indirect holding in S2 Ltd is 49% which is insufficient for H Ltd and S2 Ltd to be associates

D   Assuming all of the companies are still actively trading, there are three associates   LO 5b

54   Mountain Ltd's parent company has two other wholly owned subsidiaries. Mountain Ltd prepared its first set of accounts for the six months to 31 January 2015.

Select which of the following options correctly identifies the limits for Mountain Ltd for corporation tax purposes for the six months ended 31 January 2015.

A   £375,000 and £75,000
B   £250,000 and £50,000
C   £750,000 and £150,000
D   £187,500 and £37,500   LO 5b

55   Hill Ltd has no associated companies and taxable total profits of £1,000,000 for the year ended 31 March 2015. During the year Hill Ltd received gross exempt dividends from UK companies of £50,000.

Select which of the following options correctly identifies the amount of marginal relief available to Hill Ltd for the year ended 31 March 2015.

A   £0
B   £1,071
C   £1,250
D   £1,190   LO 5d

56   Precipice plc, a company with no associates, has produced the following results for the year ended 31 March 2015:

	£
Trading income	4,000,000
Chargeable gains	25,000
Interest receivable	95,000
Qualifying donations (of which £35,000 accrued at the year end)	50,000

Select which of the following options correctly identifies the corporation tax payable by Precipice plc for its year ended 31 March 2015.

A   £821,000
B   £854,700
C   £862,050
D   £814,000   LO 5d

57 Tor plc had taxable total profits of £1,410,000 for the year ended 30 November 2014. Tor plc has no associated companies. During this accounting period, Tor plc received no cash dividends.

Select which of the following options correctly identifies the amount of corporation tax payable by Tor plc for the year ended 30 November 2014.

A   £305,500
B   £305,125
C   £295,875
D   £282,000   LO 5d

58 Puy Ltd drew up accounts for the nine month period to 30 June 2014. The company pays interest on its £600,000 5% debenture stock annually on 31 December.

Select which of the following options correctly identifies the amount of interest allowable for tax purposes for the nine months ended 30 June 2014.

A   £24,000
B   £22,500
C   £30,000
D   Nil   LO 5c

59 Select which one of the following statements about corporation tax is true.

A   A company which is not incorporated in the UK nor centrally managed and controlled in the UK, will still be liable to UK corporation tax on its worldwide profits.

B   A company which is not incorporated in the UK will never be liable to UK corporation tax on its worldwide profits.

C   A company which is not centrally managed and controlled in the UK will never be liable to UK corporation tax on its worldwide profits.

D   A company which is incorporated in the UK but not centrally managed and controlled in the UK, will still be liable to UK corporation tax on its worldwide profits.   LO 1d

60 Esquilino plc has recently begun to rent out the top floor of its office building; the other two floors are used in its trade. Building running costs of £3,000 have been incurred for the year ended 31 December 2014. In addition interest on the loan to purchase the building was £3,900 for the year.

Select which of the following options correctly identifies the amount of costs in relation to the building which will be an allowable deduction against trading income for the year ended 31 December 2014.

A   £2,300
B   £3,000
C   £4,600
D   £6,900   LO 5c

61 Jaffrey Ltd is a UK resident trading company that made various disposals during the year ended 31 March 2015.

Select how the resulting gains or losses should be treated in the corporation tax computation of Jaffrey Ltd for the year ended 31 March 2015.

Loss of £5,900 on the sale of two cars used in the business. Each car cost and was sold for more than £6,000

    A   Chargeable gain

    B   Exempt

    C   Allowable capital loss

Gain of £86,000 on the sale of an investment property

    D   Chargeable gain

    E   Exempt

    F   Allowable capital loss   LO 4a

---

62 Ardent Ltd bought a factory on 12 February 1996 for £165,000. At acquisition, professional fees were £2,450 and stamp duty land tax was £1,650. In May 2001 an extension was added to the factory at a cost of £23,000.

In October 2014 Ardent Ltd sold the factory, which had always been used in its trade, for £312,000. Prior to the sale, Ardent Ltd repaired water damage on one wall at a total cost of £3,000.

Calculate the unindexed gain on the sale of the factory.

Unindexed gain   £ ☐

Enter a whole number WITHOUT the £ sign   LO 4b

---

63 Turner Ltd has included the following items in its profit before tax for the year ended 31 December 2014. For each item, select the adjustment that must be made to arrive at the trading income for the year ended 31 December 2014.

Depreciation of the office building

    A   Add back

    B   Deduct

    C   No adjustment

Entertaining staff at a party, which cost £85 per head

    D   Add back

    E   Deduct

    F   No adjustment   LO 5c

---

64 Select which **two** of the following items are deductible in arriving at the trading income of a UK company which manufactures furniture.

    A   Employer's national insurance contributions

    B   Gift of a £15 bottle of wine to a customer

    C   Interest on a loan taken out to purchase shares in a subsidiary

    D   Interest on overdue corporation tax

    E   Replacement of roof tiles on the company's head office building   LO 5c

65 Worrall Ltd purchased the following items during the year ended 31 March 2015.

Car used 25% for business purposes by the managing director £16,000
Computer £6,900
Low emission car £13,500

The balance on the main pool on 1 April 2014 was £54,000.

The managing director's car has CO_2 emissions of 120g/km.

Calculate the maximum capital allowances available to Worrall Ltd on the low emission car for the year ended 31 March 2015.

Capital allowances on the low emission car £ _____

Enter a whole number WITHOUT the £ sign LO 5c

---

66 Worrall Ltd purchased the following items during the year ended 31 March 2015.

Car used 20% for business purposes by the managing director £16,000
Computer £6,900
Low emission car £13,500

The balance on the main pool on 1 April 2014 was £54,000.

The managing director's car has CO_2 emissions of 120g/km.

Calculate the maximum capital allowances available to Worrall Ltd on the computer for the year ended 31 March 2015.

Capital allowances on the computer £ _____

Enter a whole number WITHOUT the £ sign LO 5c

---

67 Worrall Ltd purchased the following items during the year ended 31 March 2015.

Car used 20% for business purposes by the managing director £16,000
Computer £6,900
Low emission car £13,500

The balance on the main pool on 1 April 2014 was £54,000.

The managing director's car has CO_2 emissions of 120g/km.

Calculate the maximum capital allowances available to Worrall Ltd on the main pool for the year ended 31 March 2015.

Capital allowances on the main pool £ _____

Enter a whole number WITHOUT the £ sign LO 5c

---

68 Select which **two** of the following items are treated as a profit or loss on non-trading loan relationships for Bright Ltd.

A   Bank overdraft interest

B   Finance lease interest payable on the purchase of a company car for one of Bright Ltd's employees

C   Interest payable on a loan to purchase a factory which is used to manufacture Bright Ltd's goods

D   Interest payable on a loan to purchase an investment property

E   Interest payable on a loan to purchase shares in Dim Ltd, another trading company   LO 5d

69 Walters Ltd has taxable total profits of £230,000 for the year ended 31 March 2015. However, this figure is before the effect of the following items, which were omitted from the financial statements.

Select the effect of each item on Walters Ltd's taxable total profits.

Qualifying donations to charity

A   Increase

B   Decrease

C   No effect

Recovery of previously written off trade debts

D   Increase

E   Decrease

F   No effect   LO 5c/5d

70 Campo Ltd has taxable total profits of £225,677 for the year ended 31 December 2014. During November 2014 it received exempt dividends from UK companies of £85,000 of which £12,000 were received from an 80% subsidiary.

Select which of the following is Campo Ltd's augmented profits for the year ended 31 December 2014.

A   £225,677

B   £306,788

C   £310,677

D   £320,121   LO 5b/5d

71 Rhodes Ltd has taxable total profits for the nine-month period ended 31 March 2015 of £1,088,600. The company received no franked investment income during the period.

Calculate the corporation tax payable by Rhodes Ltd for the period ended 31 March 2015.

Corporation tax payable   £ _____

Enter a whole number WITHOUT the £ sign   LO 5d

72 Lam Ltd commenced trading on 1 February 2013 and had the following periods of account:

1 February 2013 to 31 July 2014

1 August 2014 to 30 April 2015 (when the trade ceased)

Its first corporation tax accounting period was

A   1 February 2013 to 31 July 2013

B   1 February 2013 to 31 January 2014

C   1 February 2013 to 30 April 2014

D   1 February 2013 to 31 July 2014   LO 5a

73 Jam Ltd has no associated companies and taxable total profits of £260,000 for the year ended 31 December 2014. During the accounting period Jam Ltd received gross exempt dividends from UK companies of £20,000.

Calculate the corporation tax payable by Jam Ltd for the year ended 31 December 2014.

Corporation tax payable   £ _____

Enter a whole number WITHOUT the £ sign   LO 5d

74 Alpha Ltd has taxable total profits for the ten-month period ended 30 September 2014 of
    £1,370,000. The company received no franked investment income during the period.

    Select which of the following options correctly identifies the amount of corporation tax payable by
    Alpha Ltd for the period ended 30 September 2014.

    A   £274,000
    B   £248,883
    C   £287,700
    D   £298,660   LO 5d

Chapter 11: Value added tax

1   Clementine orders some goods from Forty-Niner plc on 1 May. They are despatched on 8 May. On 4 June Clementine receives the respective invoice dated 2 June. Her payment arrives at the company on 7 June. Forty-Niner plc does not operate the cash accounting scheme.

Select which one of the following options correctly identifies the tax point for the transaction.

A   1 May
B   8 May
C   2 June
D   7 June   LO 6d

2   Matilda has been a VAT-registered trader for a number of years and has recently purchased various items for use in her trade.

Select the item on which Matilda **cannot** recover the input tax.

A   Van accessories purchased a year ago
B   Fixed partitions for use in the office
C   A motorcycle for business deliveries
D   Entertaining costs of UK business customers   LO 6e

3   James, a trader, wishes to register voluntarily for VAT.

Select which of the following options correctly identifies what James must do, in addition to completing form VAT1, in order to be so registered.

A   Demonstrate to HMRC that he intends to make either zero or standard rated supplies or both
B   Demonstrate to HMRC that he will make only zero rated supplies
C   Demonstrate to HMRC that he will make only exempt supplies
D   Demonstrate to HMRC that his sole intention for registering is to recover input tax   LO 6c

4   Bob, who is not registered for VAT, has just completed 12 months' trading, the turnover details for the past year being as follows.

	£
Exempt supplies	22,500
Standard rated supplies	55,500
Zero rated supplies	26,500

Select which of the following options correctly identifies Bob's liability to register for VAT.

A   He is not required to register
B   He must register, based on turnover of exempt and standard rated supplies
C   He must register, based on turnover of standard and zero rated supplies
D   He must register, based on turnover of exempt, standard and zero rated supplies   LO 6c

5   Charles, a VAT-registered trader, invoices Bronco Ltd in November 2014 for standard rated supplies of £1,000, excluding VAT.

The following settlement discounts are offered.

Payment within	Discount
7 days	10%
14 days	5%
21 days	2.5%

Bronco Ltd, whose normal credit term is 21 days, agrees beforehand to settle the invoice within 14 days, but actually takes 28 days.

Select which of the following options correctly identifies the amount of VAT which Charles should have charged on the invoice.

    A   £180
    B   £195
    C   £190
    D   £200

LO 6e

6   Viking Raiders Ltd commenced trading on 1 January 2014. Details of the company's recent taxable turnover is as follows.

2014	£	2015 (forecast figures)	£
January	720	January	12,970
February	1,220	February	12,960
March	2,250	March	10,770
April	2,490	April	11,860
May	3,890		
June	4,620		
July	5,870		
August	5,890		
September	5,920		
October	6,170		
November	8,800		
December	10,270		

Select which of the following options correctly identifies the date by which Viking Raiders Ltd must notify HMRC of its liability to register.

    A   28 February 2015
    B   30 March 2015
    C   31 March 2015
    D   1 April 2015

LO 6c

7   John works for Dunn plc and is provided with a company car with a list price of £16,000 and CO_2 emissions of 178g/km. The company reimburses his private and business petrol. The relevant VAT inclusive fuel scale rate is £391 per quarter.

Select which of the following options correctly identifies the output VAT charge per quarter.

    A   £0
    B   £65.17
    C   £78.20
    D   £391.00

LO 6e

8   Ralph is a salesman who incurred the following expenditure on a business trip.

	Net £	VAT £	Gross £
Hotel accommodation paid by him and reimbursed by his employer	320	64	384
Subsistence meals paid out of a flat rate expense allowance	200	40	240

Select which of the following options correctly identifies the amount of deductible input tax to be shown on the employer's VAT return.

A   £0
B   £40
C   £64
D   £104   LO 6e

9   Paint Ltd incurred the following capital expenditure (including VAT).

	£	
New car for salesman	12,810	(80% business use)
New motor van	9,450	
Second-hand container lorry	23,100	

Select which of the following options correctly identifies the amount of VAT that can be reclaimed in respect of the above.

A   £3,850
B   £5,425
C   £7,133
D   £7,560   LO 6e

10   Where a supply is made, a taxable person can, in respect of a default by a debtor, claim a refund of the relevant VAT if certain conditions are fulfilled.

Select which of the following options is **not** one of the conditions required.

A   The debtor must be formally insolvent.
B   A period of six months must have elapsed since the time of the supply and due date of payment.
C   Output tax on the supply has been accounted for and paid.
D   The debt has been written off as a bad debt in the accounts.   LO 6e

11   Tariq ordered some goods from Rumpole Ltd, which issued a VAT invoice on 1 February. As payment for the goods, Tariq sent a cheque which Rumpole Ltd received on 3 February. The goods were despatched on 8 February and received by Tariq on 10 February. Rumpole Ltd is not a member of the cash accounting scheme.

Select which of the following options correctly identifies the tax point for the supply.

A   1 February
B   3 February
C   8 February
D   10 February   LO 6d

12   Quentin, who is registered for VAT, supplies computer hardware and related support services.

On 28 March 2014 he gave a new laptop to his sister. The laptop cost the business £2,500 (excluding VAT) in January 2014 but the same model could have been purchased for £2,000 on 28 March 2014 (excluding VAT).

Select which of the following options correctly identifies the amount of output VAT that Quentin should include in his VAT return in respect of the above transaction.

A   £333.33
B   £400.00
C   £416.67
D   £500.00

LO 6e

13   Valerie is a sole trader running two separate businesses – a wholesale fabric business and a clothes retail business. She is also senior partner in a firm of interior designers. All three businesses have a taxable turnover in excess of £100,000.

Select which of the following options correctly identifies the maximum number of VAT registrations to which she will be a party.

A   One
B   Two
C   Three
D   She may elect for two or three

LO 6c

14   Cross plc issues an invoice in February 2015 as follows.

	£
Goods	1,800
Less trade discount	(180)
Cash discount (only available if the invoice is settled within 30 days)	(108)
Cash to pay within 30 days	1,512

Select which of the following options correctly identifies the amount of VAT that should be shown on the invoice.

A   £360.00
B   £338.40
C   £302.40
D   £324.00

LO 6e

15   Priti purchases goods from Kuldip as follows.

1   Kuldip receives payment for goods on 4 May

2   Kuldip despatches the goods on 8 May

3   Priti receives the goods on 12 May

4   Kuldip issues an invoice on 17 May

Kuldip does not operate the cash accounting scheme.

Select which of the following options correctly identifies the tax point for this supply.

A   4 May

B   8 May

C   12 May

D   17 May

LO 6d

16   Priscilla started trading in the winter of 2014 but did not register for VAT because she expected that her turnover would be below the registration limits. On 31 May 2015 she realised that her future taxable turnover would exceed £81,000 in the next 30 days alone.

Select the date by which she must notify HMRC that she is liable to be registered for VAT.

A   31 May 2015

B   29 June 2015

C   1 July 2015

Select the date from which she must charge VAT on her taxable supplies.

D   31 May 2015

E   30 June 2015

F   1 July 2015   LO 6c

17   Paola, who is registered for VAT, runs a chauffeur-driven car hire service. In the quarter ended 31 March 2015 she lent a car and chauffeur to her cousin, to drive him to the airport. In the same quarter Paola arranged for a car and chauffeur to drive her to the church for her wedding.

Select which of the following options correctly identifies which of these, if any, will be treated as a supply of services for VAT purposes.

A   Neither
B   Loan of car to her cousin only
C   Use of car for her wedding only
D   Both   LO 6a

18   Diane, a VAT registered trader who is not a member of the cash accounting scheme, supplies some goods to a customer. The goods are despatched on 27 March. Diane's VAT accounting period ends on 31 March. An invoice is issued on 2 April and payment is received on 4 April.

Select which of the following options correctly identifies the date of the tax point.

A   27 March
B   31 March
C   2 April
D   4 April   LO 6d

19   Walton Ltd, a manufacturing company which is registered for VAT, purchased a motor car for £10,470 (which included £160 for the road fund licence) inclusive of VAT. The car is used by one of the employees for business and private use.

Select which of the following options correctly identifies the amount which should be included in the capital allowance computation as the acquisition cost of this vehicle?

A   £8,592
B   £8,725
C   £10,310
D   £10,470   LO 6b

20 Select which of the following options is always a condition which must be fulfilled if input tax on the purchase of goods from a VAT registered person is to be recovered.

A   Payment has been made for the goods
B   A tax invoice is held
C   The supplier has been paid
D   The goods have been resold to a customer

LO 6e

21 Chris, who is registered for VAT, runs a large computer programming business in Stafford. During the quarter ended 30 June 2014 he spent £240 on his lunches taken locally and £480 on his lunches taken in Glasgow while on business trips there. Both figures include VAT.

Select which of the following options correctly identifies the amount of VAT Chris may claim as input tax.

A   £0
B   £40
C   £80
D   £120

LO 6e

22 Parminder runs two separate businesses. The first business is a clothes repair service which has taxable supplies of £35,000 per annum. The second business is a carwash service which has taxable supplies of £245,000 per annum. Both businesses are run by Parminder as a sole trader.

Select which of the following options correctly identifies which of the businesses is relevant in determining whether Parminder should register for VAT.

A   Both businesses
B   The clothes repair service
C   The car-wash service
D   Neither business

LO 6c

23 Sheep plc commenced to trade on 1 December 2014. On 1 February 2015 it won a contract to supply goods on 15 February 2015 worth £350,000.

Select the date by which Sheep plc must notify HMRC that it is liable to be registered for VAT.

A   28 February

B   2 March

C   17 March

Select the date from which Sheep plc must charge VAT on its taxable supplies.

D   1 February

E   28 February

F   1 March

LO 6c

24 Cow plc has been trading for many years and has always been VAT registered. On 1 March 2015 it ceased to make zero rated supplies. Cow plc is now a wholly exempt trader with annual supplies of £84,000 on average.

Select which of the following options correctly identifies what action Cow plc must now take in relation to its VAT registration.

A No action need be taken as the company is still making supplies in excess of £81,000.

B Deregistration will be effective immediately and must be notified by 2 March 2015.

C Deregistration will be effective immediately and must be notified by 30 March 2015.

D No action need be taken as the company is still making supplies in excess of £79,000.   LO 6c

25 Gobble plc made the following two standard rated supplies during July 2014:

Clothes (exclusive of VAT)	£400
Material (inclusive of VAT)	£514

Select which of the following options correctly identifies the total output VAT collected.

A £169.47
B £165.67
C £182.80
D £152.33   LO 6e

26 In December 2014, Moo plc makes a standard rated supply of goods and issues an invoice for £1,000 plus VAT to Ferdinand. A 4% discount is offered if payment is received within 17 days of the invoice date. In actual fact, Ferdinand took 18 days to pay.

What is the correct amount of output VAT to be charged?   £ [   ]

Enter a whole number WITHOUT the £ sign   LO 6e

27 Courgette Ltd provides Samuel with a company car with CO_2 emissions of 232g/km and fuel for both business and private mileage. Courgette Ltd claims back all the input tax relating to its fuel. During the quarter ended 31 December 2014 Courgette Ltd pays £634 (including VAT) for Samuel's fuel. The relevant VAT inclusive fuel scale rate is £548.

What is the amount of output VAT to be accounted for?   £ [   ]

Enter a whole number WITHOUT the £ sign   LO 6e

28 From the following list of purchases, select those TWO items for which the input VAT is **always** wholly irrecoverable.

A UK client entertaining
B Fuel in company pool cars
C Capital item still used exclusively for business use but purchased two months pre-registration
D Gifts of goods to customers
E Company car for employee use which is a taxable benefit for income tax purposes   LO 6e

29 In his first year of trading to 31 December 2014, Wayne's taxable turnover from his business was £3,700 each month.

For the first seven months of 2015 his taxable turnover was as follows:

	£
January 2015	6,100
February 2015	6,800
March 2015	7,500
April 2015	11,900
May 2015	13,200
June 2015	14,900
July 2015	13,000

Select which of the following options correctly identifies the date by which Wayne must notify HMRC of his liability to register for VAT.

A   30 May 2015
B   30 June 2015
C   30 July 2015
D   30 August 2015

LO 6c

30 Benedict commenced to trade on 1 August 2014 repairing electrical equipment and applied to register for VAT with effect from 1 December 2014. Prior to registration he had incurred VAT as follows.

	£
Van purchased on 3 May 2014 still in use at 30 November 2014	500
Accountancy fees on invoice dated 5 September 2014	30
Stock of spare parts as at 30 November 2014	240

Select which of the following options correctly identifies the amount of VAT Benedict can reclaim in respect of these items.

A   £770
B   £740
C   £270
D   £240

LO 6e

31 Select which of the following statements about VAT is true.

A   A trader who makes only exempt supplies may register for VAT.

B   VAT is charged on zero rated supplies.

C   VAT on standard rated supplies is always charged at 5%.

D   A trader making taxable supplies may only register for VAT once supplies exceed the VAT registration threshold.

LO 6b/6c

32 Michael commenced trading as a cabinet maker on 1 October 2013. His quarterly turnover (spread evenly over the quarter) is as follows.

Quarter ended	£
31 December 2013	12,000
31 March 2014	13,200
30 June 2014	16,500
30 September 2014	26,700
31 December 2014	32,700
31 March 2015	35,000

Select which of the following options correctly identifies the date by which Michael must notify HMRC of his liability to register for VAT.

A 30 December 2014
B 31 December 2014
C 30 January 2015
D 31 January 2015   LO 6c

33 Miranda's taxable sales have dropped to £30,000 pa and forecast annual sales are expected to be between £30,000 – £40,000.

Select which of the following options correctly identifies the VAT implications for Miranda.

A Miranda must deregister and will need to repay input VAT recovered on stock and capital items still held at deregistration.

B Miranda must deregister and will need to repay input VAT recovered on stock and capital items still held at deregistration where the input VAT exceeds £1,000.

C Miranda may choose to deregister but would then need to repay input VAT recovered on stock and capital items still held at deregistration if the input VAT exceeds £1,000.

D Miranda may choose to deregister but would then need to repay input VAT recovered on stock and capital items still held at deregistration.   LO 6c

34 Select which of the following is **not** a deemed supply for VAT purposes.

A Sale of goods on hire purchase.
B Gifts of business assets worth £100 each to a customer.
C Gifts of services worth £100 each to a customer.
D Drawings of stock by the proprietor of a business.   LO 6a

35 Kevin is a VAT registered trader who has suffered input tax as follows on purchases in the past month.

	£
Television for Kevin's wife	350
Machine for business use (Kevin has lost the VAT receipt)	989
Office stationery	256

Select which of the following correctly identifies the amount of input tax Kevin may recover on these items.

A £256
B £989
C £1,245
D £1,595   LO 6e

36 Select which of the following statements about VAT is true.

 A Where discounts are offered VAT should be calculated based on those discounts actually obtained rather than those available.

 B A gift of business services is not a taxable supply.

 C A supply of a business asset used for private purposes is not a taxable supply.

 D VAT fuel scale charges give the recoverable input VAT on private fuel purchases. LO 6b/6e

37 Flight plc is VAT registered but is not a member of the cash accounting scheme. A major customer of Flight plc went into liquidation today and there is little hope of its debt being recovered. The invoice was issued on 1 August 2014 with a credit agreement of payment by the end of the month. The associated output VAT was paid to HMRC in the quarter ended 31 October 2014 return. The debt will be written off in Flight plc's accounts on 31 March 2015.

Assuming it is now 1 January 2015 select which of the following options correctly identifies the earliest date the output VAT could be reclaimed from HMRC.

 A 1 January 2015
 B 1 February 2015
 C 28 February 2015
 D 31 March 2015 LO 6e

38 Sunil ordered some goods from Grumpy Ltd, which issued a VAT invoice on 1 September. Sunil sent a cheque for the goods which Grumpy Ltd received on 3 September. The goods were despatched on 8 September and received by Sunil on 10 September. Grumpy Ltd is not a member of the cash accounting scheme.

Select which of the following options correctly identifies the tax point for the supply.

 A 1 September
 B 3 September
 C 8 September
 D 10 September LO 6d

39 Tien orders some goods on sale or return from Spice Ltd on 1 October. They are despatched on 9 October. Tien adopts the goods on 1 November. Tien then receives the invoice for the goods dated 20 November. Spice Ltd receives payment for the goods on 29 December.

The actual tax point of the transaction is

 A 1 October
 B 9 October
 C 1 November
 D 20 November LO 6d

40 Ahsan orders some goods from Land Ltd on 1 October. They are despatched on 18 October. Ahsan then receives the invoice for the goods dated 29 October. Land Ltd receives payment for the goods on 7 December. Ahsan is not a member of the cash accounting scheme.

The actual tax point of the transaction is

 A 1 October
 B 18 October
 C 29 October
 D 7 December LO 6d

41 Disco Ltd intends to register voluntarily for VAT.

Identify which of the following statements is correct.

A   Disco Ltd must be expecting to be in a repayment position.
B   Disco Ltd must not be making any exempt supplies.
C   Disco Ltd must be making or intending to make some taxable supplies.
D   Disco Ltd must be expecting to exceed the VAT threshold within the next 12 months.   LO 6c

42 Tambourine Ltd makes standard rated supplies. At the end of October 2014 its taxable turnover in the previous 12 months exceeds £81,000 for the first time. Its turnover is expected to rise gradually.

The company is required to notify HMRC of its liability to register by

A   1 November 2014

B   30 November 2014

C   1 December 2014

Registration takes effect from

D   1 November 2014

E   30 November 2014

F   1 December 2014   LO 6c

43 Arthur, who is not registered for VAT, has just completed 12 months' trading. The turnover for the trading year is as follows.

	£
Exempt supplies	12,300
Taxable supplies	69,250

Additionally Arthur sold an item of machinery (standard rated) for £12,000.

Based on the above information, does Arthur have any liability to register for VAT?

A   Yes, based on exempt and taxable supplies of normal trading.
B   Yes, based on taxable supplies of normal trading, plus the sale of machinery.
C   No, based on taxable supplies of normal trading.
D   Yes, based on exempt and taxable supplies of normal trading, plus the sale of machinery. LO 6c

44 Abida is a salesman who incurred the following expenditure during his work.

	Net £	VAT £	Gross £
Hotel accommodation reimbursed to him by his employers	320	64	384
Meals paid out of his salary	200	40	240

In addition his employer purchased a laptop computer for Abida to use as an essential part of his job. The employer agreed 10% personal use for this equipment which had cost £1,080 (including VAT of £180).

How much may be shown as net deductible input tax on the employer's VAT return?

A   £226
B   £244
C   £266
D   £284   LO 6e

45   Books Ltd incurred the following capital expenditure (including VAT).

	£
Car for salesman used for business and private purposes	15,750
Delivery van	10,080

How much VAT can be reclaimed in respect of the above?

A   £2,016
B   £1,680
C   £2,625
D   £4,305

LO 6e

46   Identify whether the following are correct conditions for the reclaim of output tax as bad debt relief.

A period of six months has elapsed since the goods were supplied.

A   Correct

B   Incorrect

Tax on the supply has been accounted for and paid.

C   Correct

D   Incorrect

The bad debt claim must be made within 6 years of becoming eligible for relief.

E   Correct

F   Incorrect

LO 6e

47   Music Ltd has just received the following invoice from a supplier (all figures exclude VAT).

	£
Musical equipment	6,400
Less 10 % discount for settlement within 14 days	(640)
Cash to pay if settled within 14 days	5,760

If payment is made within 21 days the discount is reduced to 5%.

Music Ltd has a policy of paying one month after being invoiced.

What is the correct amount of VAT that should be shown on the invoice?

A   £960
B   £1,152
C   £1,216
D   £1,280

LO 6e

48   Peter purchases goods from John. Peter paid for the goods when he ordered them on 3 April. John made the goods available to Peter on 7 April, but Peter did not collect them until 11 April. John issued the invoice on 16 April.

What is the actual tax point for this supply?

A   3 April
B   7 April
C   11 April
D   16 April

LO 6d

49 Identify whether each of the following is a taxable supply of services.

Steve, who is registered for VAT, runs a plant hire company. In the quarter ended 31 March 2015 he let his brother use a digger at no charge.

A   Taxable

B   Not taxable

In the quarter to 30 June 2015 he used the same digger to help dig the foundations for the extension being built onto his house.

C   Taxable

D   Not taxable   LO 6a

50 Block Ltd, a building company which is registered for VAT, purchased a motor car for use by the sales director for £25,380 (including £705 for the factory fitted satellite navigation), inclusive of VAT. The car is used 20% privately by the sales director.

What is the cost to the company of the vehicle for capital allowance purposes?

A   £25,380
B   £24,675
C   £21,150
D   £20,563   LO 6b

51 Charlie has a shop selling women's clothing. She gave a coat that she had bought for £120 to her sister. She would have sold the coat in the shop for £200. All figures are VAT-inclusive.

The value of the coat for VAT purposes is

A   £200.00
B   £166.67
C   £120.00
D   £100.00   LO 6b

52 Eve has a company car with CO_2 emissions of 216g/km provided by her employer Apples Ltd. Apples Ltd paid petrol invoices totalling £945 inclusive of VAT for Eve's car in the quarter to 31 October 2014. The VAT inclusive quarterly scale rate for a car like Eve's is £517.

What is the net VAT position relating to Eve's car in the quarter to 31 October 2014?

A   £86.17 payable
B   £157.50 reclaimable
C   £71.33 payable
D   £71.33 reclaimable   LO 6e

53 Gertrude has a quarter ended 31 March 2015. Her normal payment terms are one calendar month after invoice date. Identify whether bad debt relief can be claimed in respect of the following amounts owed to Gertrude as at 31 March 2015.

Wood Ltd still owes £5,000 from an invoice issued on 30 June 2014. Gertrude still believes that the amount will be paid in full and so it has not been written off in the accounts.

A   Bad debt relief can be claimed

B   Bad debt relief cannot be claimed

Trees Ltd owes £2,000 from an invoice issued on 15 September 2014. Gertrude does not expect payment of this debt and has written it off in the accounts.

C   Bad debt relief can be claimed

D   Bad debt relief cannot be claimed   LO 6e

54 Jacob, who is VAT registered, opened a new shop selling electrical supplies. He took goods valued at £230 for use in his own house and sent out a sample worth £12 to each of 200 potential new customers.

Which of the following statements is correct?

A   Only the goods used in Jacob's house are a taxable supply.
B   Only the samples sent to potential customers are a taxable supply.
C   Both are taxable supplies.
D   Neither are taxable supplies.   LO 6a

55 Identify whether each of the following statements is correct.

A business making £45,000 of standard rated supplies and £37,000 of exempt supplies is required to register for VAT

A   Correct

B   Incorrect

A business making £82,000 of zero rated supplies only does not have to become VAT registered

C   Correct

D   Incorrect   LO 6c

56 Lancashire Ltd commenced trading on 1 January 2014. The company's taxable turnover was £4,900 per month for the first 6 months, rising to £7,600 per month for the next six months. In January 2015 the turnover increased to £11,000 per month.

Lancashire Ltd must start to charge VAT on its supplies from

A   31 January 2015
B   28 February 2015
C   1 March 2015
D   2 March 2015   LO 6c

57　Yorks Ltd began trading on 1 January 2015, anticipating taxable turnover of £83,000 per month.

It must notify HMRC of its liability to register for VAT by

A　1 January 2015

B　30 January 2015

C　31 January 2015

The company's VAT registration is effective from

D　1 January 2015

E　30 January 2015

F　31 January 2015　　　　　　　　　　　　　　　　　　　　　　　　　　　LO 6c

58　Maddie is registered for VAT and makes standard rated supplies only. Maddie sold some goods to Julie for £76 without charging any VAT because Maddie believed that the goods were exempt from VAT.

Maddie has now discovered that VAT should have been charged on this sale.

Select how much VAT is payable on this sale and by whom.

The amount of VAT payable is

A　£12.67

B　£15.20

The VAT is payable by

C　Maddie

D　Julie　　　　　　　　　　　　　　　　　　　　　　　　　　　　　　LO 1d/6e

59　Harry commenced trading on 1 September 2014. His monthly turnover for the first 18 months of trade is as follows.

	Per month (excluding VAT) £
Turnover	
Standard rated supplies	4,600
Zero rated supplies	1,900
Exempt supplies	500
	6,000

On 1 May 2015, Harry sold surplus office machinery for £3,500 (excluding VAT).

Select whether the following supplies should be included in order to determine when the VAT registration limit of £81,000 is first exceeded by Harry's business.

Exempt supplies

A　Include

B　Do not include

Supply of surplus office machinery

C　Include

D　Do not include　　　　　　　　　　　　　　　　　　　　　　　　　　LO 6c

60   Skating Ltd is a VAT registered company that only makes standard rated supplies.

Select the extent to which the input tax is recoverable on the following VAT-inclusive costs incurred by Skating Ltd.

£15,000 for the purchase of a new machine. The VAT invoice has been lost and cannot be replaced

A   Fully recoverable

B   Partially recoverable

C   Not recoverable

Purchase of a car for a salesman for £20,000. The car is used 60% for business purposes

D   Fully recoverable

E   Partially recoverable

F   Not recoverable   LO 6e

---

61   Jack is a VAT registered trader making only standard rated supplies. Jack received an order from a customer on 20 February 2015 and dispatched the goods on the same day. Included with the order was payment of a 10% deposit of £1,150 including VAT.

An invoice for the full amount of £11,500 including VAT was issued on 1 March 2015. The balancing payment of £10,350 was received on 10 April 2015.

Assuming that Jack does not operate the cash accounting scheme, calculate how much output tax must be accounted for on the following VAT returns:

Quarter to 28 February 2015

A   £0

B   £192

C   £1,150

Quarter to 31 May 2015

D   £0

E   £1,725

F   £1,917   LO 6e

---

62   David is registered for VAT. David sold goods to George for £100 without charging any VAT. George had assured him that the goods were exempt from VAT. David later discovered that the standard rate of VAT should have been charged on this sale.

Select how much VAT is payable on this sale and by whom.

The amount of VAT payable is

A   £16.67

B   £20.00

The VAT is payable by

C   David

D   George   LO 1d/6e

63 Select which **two** of the following statements are correct in relation to registering for VAT.

  A   A trader can voluntarily register for VAT if he makes only exempt supplies

  B   A trader can voluntarily register for VAT if he makes only zero rated supplies

  C   A trader making both zero rated and standard rated supplies is required to register only if the level of taxable supplies exceeds the VAT registration limit

  D   A trader making exempt supplies must register for VAT if his supplies exceed the VAT registration limit

  LO 6c

64 Branimir is registered for VAT and is preparing his VAT return for the three-month period ended 31 March 2015. During this period he made zero rated supplies of £23,000 and standard rated supplies of £29,560. These figures are VAT exclusive.

  Branimir incurred input tax related to the zero rated supplies of £2,130 and input tax related to the standard rated supplies of £900. Branimir also paid salaries of £5,800 for the three-month period which relate to the business as a whole.

  Calculate how much output VAT Branimir should account for on his VAT return for the three months ended 31 March 2015.

  Output VAT   £ [   ]

  Enter a whole number WITHOUT the £ sign

  LO 6e

65 Branimir is registered for VAT and is preparing his VAT return for the three-month period ended 31 March 2015. During this period he made zero rated supplies of £23,000 and standard rated supplies of £29,560. These figures are VAT exclusive.

  Branimir incurred input tax related to the zero rated supplies of £2,130 and input tax related to the standard rated supplies of £900. Branimir also paid salaries of £5,800 for the three-month period which relate to the business as a whole.

  Calculate how much input VAT Branimir should account for on his VAT return for the three months ended 31 March 2015.

  Input VAT   £ [   ]

  Enter a whole number WITHOUT the £ sign

  LO 6e

66 Eloise commenced business as a sole trader on 1 January 2014 making only taxable supplies. Her turnover in the first 18 months of trade was as follows.

1 January 2014 to 31 August 2014	£6,150 per month
September and October 2014	£10,500 per month
From November 2014 onwards	£11,000 per month

  Select the date by which Eloise should have notified HMRC that she was required to become VAT registered in order to avoid a late registration penalty.

  A   1 January 2014
  B   30 November 2014
  C   30 December 2014
  D   30 January 2015

  LO 6c

1   Lavender Ltd has prepared its VAT return for the quarter ended 31 March 2015.

Select which of the following options correctly identifies the date by which Lavender Ltd should submit its VAT return for the quarter ended 31 March 2015.

A   31 March 2015

B   30 April 2015

C   7 May 2015

Select which of the following options correctly identifies the date by which Lavender Ltd should pay its VAT relating to the quarter ended 31 March 2015.

D   31 March 2015

E   30 April 2015

F   7 May 2015   LO 2d

2   Cornflower plc had an annual VAT liability in 2014 of £3,000,000. Its VAT liability for the quarter ended 31 March 2015 is £900,000.

Select which of the following options correctly identifies Cornflower plc's required VAT payments for the quarter ended 31 March 2015.

A   A single payment of £900,000
B   Three separate payments of £300,000 each
C   Two payments of £250,000 each and a balancing payment of £400,000
D   Two payments of £125,000 each and a balancing payment of £650,000   LO 6f

3   Select which of the following options correctly identifies the maximum invoice value if a trader wishes to issue a less detailed VAT invoice.

A   £50
B   £100
C   £250
D   £1,000   LO 1d

4   Which **two** of the following statements is **not** correct in relation to VAT invoices.

A   A VAT invoice must be issued to all taxable and non taxable customers.

B   A VAT invoice must contain certain details including the VAT registration number, the total VAT chargeable and a description of the goods supplied.

C   A less detailed invoice may be issued if the VAT inclusive sale proceeds are less than £150.

D   The VAT invoice is the usual record used to support a recovery of input VAT.   LO 1d

5　Dilara has a business with a year ended 31 December 2014. Dilara uses the annual accounting scheme.

Which of the following statements is correct?

A　She pays all of her VAT in one balancing payment and submits her return by 7 February 2015.

B　She pays all of her VAT in one balancing payment and submits her return by 28 February 2015.

C　She pays her VAT in 9 monthly instalments starting in April 2014 with a balancing payment and the return submitted by 7 February 2015.

D　She pays her VAT in 9 monthly instalments starting in April 2014 with a balancing payment and the return submitted by 28 February 2015.　　　　LO 6f

6　Duffey operates the annual accounting scheme for his VAT payments. He opted to make nine monthly payments during the year. His total VAT liability in the year ended 31 March 2014 was £20,000 and in the year ended 31 March 2015 is £22,500.

The final balancing payment of his VAT for the year ended 31 March 2015 is

A　£2,500 by 7 May 2015
B　£2,500 by 31 May 2015
C　£4,500 by 7 May 2015
D　£4,500 by 31 May 2015　　　　LO 6f

7　Michael is registered for VAT. He issues detailed invoices for goods sold for more than £250, and less detailed invoices for goods sold for less than £250.

Select which of the following options correctly identifies for which of these invoices, if either, Michael must retain copies.

A　Neither
B　Detailed invoices only
C　Less detailed invoices only
D　Both　　　　LO 1d

8　Select which of the following options correctly identifies the maximum permitted annual taxable turnover for a trader to join the annual accounting scheme.

A　£100,000
B　£1,350,000
C　£1,600,000
D　£150,000　　　　LO 6f

9　Select which of the following statements about the VAT payments on account scheme for substantial traders is true.

A　Under the payments on account scheme VAT is paid in quarterly instalments.

B　Under the payments on account scheme VAT is paid in instalments every other month (ie six payments per annum).

C　Each payment on account is 1/24 of the total VAT liability of the previous year.

D　The balancing amount for the year, if any, is payable two months after the year end.　　　　LO 6f

10   Select which **two** of the following statements about VAT are true.

    A   Businesses with taxable turnover greater than £2.3m must join the VAT payments on account scheme.

    B   Businesses operating the flat rate scheme apply their sector percentage to total (both taxable and exempt) VAT inclusive turnover.

    C   HMRC may grant exemption from registration to zero rated traders that have negligible amounts of input VAT.

    D   Businesses operating the annual accounting scheme must still file VAT returns every quarter.

    E   Businesses operating the cash accounting scheme cannot also join the annual accounting scheme.   LO 6f

11   Which **two** of the following statements concerning cash accounting are **not** true?

    A   VAT is accounted for on the basis of cash paid and received rather than on invoices

    B   Automatic bad debt relief is received

    C   The scheme is advantageous for businesses making only zero rated supplies

    D   The scheme is advantageous for businesses offering extended credit to customers

    E   Businesses in the scheme must leave if taxable supplies in the previous 12 months exceed £1.35m   LO 6f

12   A trader may join the annual accounting scheme where the taxable turnover in the following year is not expected to exceed £ ☐

    Enter a whole number WITHOUT the £ sign   LO 6f

13   Major plc had a VAT liability of £3m in its year ended 31 October 2014. The VAT liability for the quarter to 30 April 2015 is £800,000. Assuming the correct payments on account have been made, how much is due by 31 May 2015?

    A   £800,000
    B   £550,000
    C   £300,000
    D   £125,000   LO 6f

14   Identify which of the following is **not** a feature of the annual accounting scheme.

    A   There is a reduction in the number of VAT returns required
    B   Automatic bad debt relief is given
    C   The VAT return is due two months after the end of the year
    D   Payments on account must be made   LO 6f

15   Identify which of the following is **not** a feature of the flat rate scheme.

    A   Businesses calculate VAT due as a flat rate percentage of their VAT exclusive turnover
    B   The percentage applied depends on the type of business
    C   Businesses issue normal tax invoices to customers
    D   There is a 1% reduction in the flat rate percentage during the first year of VAT registration   LO 6f

16 Giovanna makes standard rated supplies. She voluntarily registered for VAT from her first day of trading and simultaneously joined the flat rate scheme. The flat rate percentage she must use is 11%.

She has now been trading for two years. For her latest trading quarter Giovanna had total turnover of £8,500 (exclusive of VAT). Giovanna's total purchases were £2,400 (exclusive of VAT).

Select which of the following options correctly identifies the amount of VAT payable to HMRC for Giovanna's latest trading quarter.

A   £671
B   £805
C   £935
D   £1,122   LO 6f

17 Florence Ltd is a VAT registered business which operates the cash accounting scheme. During the quarter ended 31 December 2014 it made the following purchases:

	Goods received	Date paid	Input VAT suffered £
Artwork for reception	30 November 2014	15 December 2014	1,150
Spare machinery parts	1 December 2014	13 January 2015	242
Marketing literature	1 September 2014	1 October 2014	858

Select which of the following options correctly identifies the amount of input tax Florence Ltd may recover on these items in the VAT return for the quarter ended 31 December 2014.

A   £1,150
B   £1,392
C   £2,008
D   £2,250   LO 6f

18 Gordon, a VAT registered trader who is a member of the cash accounting scheme, supplies some goods to a customer. The order is received from the customer on 5 May and the goods are despatched on 13 May. An invoice is issued on 16 May and payment is received from the customer on 4 June.

Select which of the following options correctly identifies the tax point of the supply.

A   5 May
B   13 May
C   16 May
D   4 June   LO 6d/6f

19 Tony has been VAT registered for many years, making only standard rated supplies. He is a member of the flat rate scheme for VAT. The flat rate percentage based on his trade sector is 8%.

In the quarter ended 31 March 2015 Tony made sales of £17,000 (exclusive of VAT). Tony's total purchases were £6,400 (exclusive of VAT).

Select which of the following options correctly identifies the amount of VAT payable to HMRC for the quarter ended 31 March 2015.

A   £848
B   £1,018
C   £1,360
D   £1,632   LO 6f

20   Select which **two** of the following statements are correct in relation to the flat rate scheme.

    A   A trader can join if he expects total net turnover for the next twelve months not to exceed £150,000.

    B   A trader using the flat rate scheme may also be authorised to use the annual accounting scheme.

    C   The flat rate is applied to the VAT exclusive turnover.

    D   Where a customer requires an invoice, a flat rate trader who makes wholly standard rated supplies will issue a VAT invoice showing 20% output tax.   LO 6f

21   Select which **two** of the following statements are correct in relation to the cash accounting scheme for VAT.

    A   A VAT return is completed once a year
    B   Automatic bad debt relief is given
    C   Output VAT is accounted for when cash is received from the customer
    D   Output VAT is calculated by applying a flat rate percentage to the VAT inclusive turnover
    E   VAT is paid over to HMRC each month by direct debit   LO 6f

Chapter 13: Administration of tax

1   Camilla commenced to trade in January 2014. Camilla's profit for the year ended 31 December 2014 was £56,000. She has not contacted HMRC to inform it that she has commenced to trade and has never been issued with nor completed a self assessment return.

Select which of the following options correctly identifies the latest date by which Camilla should have contacted HMRC to obtain a self assessment return.

A   5 October 2014
B   31 October 2014
C   31 January 2015
D   5 October 2015   LO 2c

2   Anne received her self assessment return relating to the year 2014/15 on 15 December 2015.

Select which of the following options correctly identifies the latest date by which Anne should submit her return online.

A   31 December 2015
B   31 January 2016
C   15 March 2016
D   31 March 2016   LO 2d

3   Andrew is an employee (not a director) of Toes Ltd with an annual salary of £50,000 and net bank interest of approximately £500 per year.

Select which of the following options correctly identifies the type of self assessment return Andrew is required to file each year.

A   Short tax return

B   Full tax return

Assuming Andrew were to leave his employment to set up in business with a turnover of £10,000 per annum, what type of self assessment return would he then be required to file each year?

C   Short tax return

D   Full tax return   LO 2c

4   Edward is an employee of Theatre Ltd with an annual salary of £66,000. In addition, Edward has run his own business for a number of years with an average annual profit of about £25,000.

Select which of the following options correctly identifies the end of the statutory retention period for Edward's records relating to the tax year ended 5 April 2015.

A   31 January 2020

B   31 January 2021

James is an employee of Stage Ltd with an annual salary of £45,000. He also owns a number of shares on which he receives dividend income in excess of £10,000 per year.

Select which of the following options correctly identifies the end of the statutory retention period for James's records relating to the tax year ended 5 April 2015.

C   31 January 2017

D   31 January 2018   LO 2a

5   Beatrice received her tax return for the tax year 2013/14 in April 2014 and filed it on 31 March 2015. She has now realised that she made a mistake in the return and wishes to amend it accordingly.

Select which of the following options correctly identifies the latest date by which the amendment can be made.

A   5 April 2016
B   30 April 2016
C   31 January 2016
D   31 March 2016   LO 2c

6   Eugenie is a higher rate taxpayer. She is an employee and has run her own business as a sole trader with profits in excess of £100,000 per annum for a number of years.

Select which of the following options correctly identifies the dates by which Eugenie's income tax not deducted at source is payable for the year 2014/15.

A   31 January 2015 and 31 July 2015
B   31 January 2015, 31 July 2015 and 31 January 2016
C   31 July 2015 and 31 January 2016
D   31 January 2016   LO 2d

7   Harry's total income tax liability for 2013/14 was £15,000 and his Class 4 NIC liability was £2,000. During 2013/14 £6,000 of his income tax liability was paid via tax deducted at source. Harry's capital gains tax liability for 2013/14 was £2,500.

What is Harry's first payment on account for 2014/15?

Payment on account   £ [   ]

Enter a whole number WITHOUT the £ sign   LO 2d

8   Sophie made the following payments of tax relating to 2014/15.

	£
1st payment on account 15 February 2015	22,000
2nd payment on account 31 August 2015	15,000
Balancing payment 30 April 2016	11,000

Select which of the following statements in relation to Sophie's payments is correct.

A   All of the payments were made late and will be liable to a penalty at 5%

B   All of the payments were made late and will be liable to interest from the due date to the day before payment plus those made more than 30 days late will be liable to a penalty at 5%

C   All of the payments were made late and will be liable to interest from the due date to the day before payment but only the balancing payment is liable to a penalty at 5%

D   All of the payments were made late and will be liable to interest from the due date to the day before payment plus a penalty at 5%   LO 2e

9   Albert commenced to trade as a sole trader on 1 July 2014.

Select which of the following options correctly identifies the latest date by which Albert should have contacted HMRC to obtain a self assessment return.

A   30 September 2014
B   5 October 2014
C   5 October 2015
D   31 January 2016   LO 2c

10   Barbara has been trading as a self-employed beautician for many years. She prepares accounts to 31 December each year.

She submitted her tax return for 2014/15 on 1 November 2015.

Until what date must she retain her business records for the year to 31 December 2014?

A   31 December 2019
B   31 December 2020
C   31 January 2020
D   31 January 2021   LO 2a

11   A notice to make a 2014/15 tax return was issued to Cuthbert on 30 September 2015.

Which **two** of the following statements correctly identify when Cuthbert must file the return?

A   By 30 November 2015 if he wants HMRC to calculate his tax
B   By 31 October 2015 if he wants HMRC to calculate his tax
C   By 31 December 2015 if he wants HMRC to calculate his tax
D   By 31 December 2015 if he wants to file online
E   By 31 January 2016 if he wants to file online   LO 2d

12   Elaine submits her 2014/15 tax return online on 1 December 2015. The return was issued on 6 May 2015.

Which **two** of the following statements are correct?

A   Elaine can amend her tax return on 15 December 2016

B   HMRC can correct an arithmetic error in her return on 29 September 2016

C   Elaine can make a claim for overpayment relief because there is an error in her return on 31 December 2018

D   HMRC can give notice of an enquiry into her return on 20 December 2016   LO 2c

13   Fred submitted his 2014/15 tax return on 1 September 2015. HMRC discovered on 1 October 2016 that Fred did not disclose a source of taxable income. HMRC believes that this was a genuine mistake (ie not careless or deliberate) by Fred and that he did not intend to avoid paying tax on the income.

If HMRC wishes to collect the unpaid tax, it must raise an assessment by 5 April [   ]

(Enter a year in the format 20XX)   LO 2c

14 Harriet's income tax liability was £28,450 for 2013/14 and £29,750 for 2014/15. PAYE of £23,400 was deducted in 2013/14 and £23,500 in 2014/15.

What payment on account of her 2014/15 tax liability should Harriet have paid on 31 July 2015?

A   £0
B   £2,475
C   £2,525
D   £3,125   LO 2d

15 Ivan's tax position for 2014/15 and the previous year is as follows.

| | 2013/14 | 2014/15 |
	£	£
Total income tax liability	15,500	17,000
Class 4 NICs	3,200	3,500
Paid under PAYE/tax credits	3,800	3,900
Payments on account made	13,000	

On 31 January 2015, to avoid interest charges under self assessment, Ivan should have paid tax of
£ [   ]

Enter a whole number WITHOUT the £ sign   LO 2d

16 John's income tax and capital gains tax liabilities for 2013/14 were £18,200 and £4,200 respectively. He paid £5,000 PAYE and payments on account for 2013/14 of £6,000.

His income tax liability for 2014/15 is £19,500 and his capital gains tax liability is £6,500.

What payment on account of his 2014/15 tax liability should John have paid on 31 July 2015?

A   £9,750
B   £7,250
C   £6,600
D   £3,000   LO 2d

17 Kurt had an income tax liability of £9,500 and a capital gains tax liability of £2,300 for 2013/14. The tax payable under self assessment for 2012/13 was £8,000.

Kurt has made the following payments in respect of his 2013/14 tax liability.

| | Cash paid |
	£
15 February 2014	3,500
29 July 2014	4,500
15 March 2015	3,800
	11,800

What is the amount of the penalties for late payment payable by Kurt in respect of the above payments?

A   £365
B   £190
C   £380
D   £590   LO 2e

18 Martha filed her 2013/14 tax return online on 5 January 2015. On 31 March 2015 HMRC issued a discovery assessment showing additional tax due of £1,500. Martha paid the tax on 15 May 2015.

Which of the following statements are true?

Interest will run on the additional liability of £1,500 from 1 April 2015 to 14 May 2015

A True
B False

A penalty of £75 is payable by Martha

C True
D False   LO 2e

19 Which of the following statements concerning the appeals procedure are true?

An appeal against a discovery assessment must be made in writing within a calendar month of the date of the assessment

A True
B False

The taxpayer must first apply for an internal review before making an appeal to the First-tier Tribunal.

C True
D False

A taxpayer can appeal against and apply to postpone the tax due under an assessment raised as a result of an enquiry into a tax return

E True
F False   LO 2f

20 Andrea's only source of income is from employment and she does not normally complete a tax return. On 1 May 2014 she sold a painting generating a chargeable gain of £100,000.

By what date must she notify HMRC of the chargeable gain, in order not to incur any penalties?

A 1 May 2015
B 5 October 2015
C 31 October 2015
D 31 January 2016   LO 2c

21 Ethel submitted her 2014/15 tax return on 1 December 2015. She omitted to include rental income from an overseas property, as she did not think that HMRC would find out about the income.

Until what date can HMRC raise a discovery assessment to collect tax on the undisclosed income?

A 5 April 2019
B 5 April 2021
C 5 April 2035
D 5 April 2036   LO 2c

22 Fred's income tax liability was £15,320 for 2013/14 and £17,480 for 2014/15. In each of these years he received £1,620 of dividend income.

Tax deducted from bank interest was £2,000 in 2013/14 and £2,500 in 2014/15.

What payment on account of his 2014/15 tax liability should Fred have paid on 31 January 2015?

A   £6,570
B   £6,660
C   £7,650
D   £7,660   LO 2d

23 Greg's tax position for 2014/15 and the previous year is as follows:

	2013/14 £	2014/15 £
Total income tax liability	23,200	24,300
Paid under PAYE/tax credits	19,000	19,200
Capital gains tax	3,200	1,200

How much tax should Greg have paid on 31 July 2015 to avoid any interest charges?

A   £0
B   £2,550
C   £2,100
D   £3,700   LO 2d

24 Harold's tax position for 2014/15 and the previous year is as follows.

	2013/14 £	2014/15 £
Total income tax liability	12,100	13,250
Class 4 NIC	3,400	3,550
Tax deducted at source	300	500

As at 30 July 2015 Harold has paid £5,500 on account of his 2014/15 tax liability.

Harold is due to make a payment on 31 July 2015. To minimise any interest charges you would advise that he makes a payment on that date of £ [   ]

Enter a whole number WITHOUT the £ sign   LO 2d

25 Ingrid had tax payable under self assessment for 2012/13 of £8,500. She submitted her income tax return for 2013/14 online on 15 February 2015. The return showed an income tax liability of £10,100 and a capital gains tax liability of £1,200. On the same date she paid the outstanding tax of £2,800.

Ingrid had made two equal payments on account totalling £8,500 on 15 January 2014 and 31 August 2014 in respect of 2013/14.

What is the amount of any penalties payable by Ingrid in respect of 2013/14?

A   £0
B   £100
C   £240
D   £2,900   LO 2e

26   A notice to submit a 2014/15 tax return was issued to Laura on 30 November 2015. When must Laura file the return by if:

She wants HMRC to calculate her tax liability?

A   28 January 2016

B   31 January 2016

C   28 February 2016

She intends to calculate her own tax liability?

D   28 January 2016

E   31 January 2016

F   28 February 2016   LO 2d

27   Asha received a gross salary of £60,000 in 2014/15. She also received property income of £700 per month from an investment property that she has held for many years. On 10 September 2015 Asha submitted her self assessment tax return for 2014/15.

Select the following time limits in relation to Asha's self assessment return for 2014/15.

Asha paying the balancing payment of tax due on the return

A   31 Jan 2016

B   10 Jun 2016

C   10 Sept 2016

D   31 Jan 2017

HMRC correcting obvious errors in Asha's return

E   31 Jan 2016

F   10 Jun 2016

G   10 Sept 2016

H   31 Jan 2017   LO 2c/2d

28   Roof Ltd has yet to pay its PAYE due for the last month of 2013/14. It has also failed to submit its P11D and P9D forms relating to 2013/14. Roof Ltd does not make payments electronically.

Select which of the following options identifies the correct due date for the PAYE relating to the final month of 2013/14.

A   14 April 2014

B   19 April 2014

Select which of the following options identifies the correct due date for the submission of P11D and P9D forms relating to 2013/14.

C   31 May 2014

D   6 July 2014   LO 2d

29   Select which of the following correctly identifies a P45 form.

    A   End of year form recording details of benefits provided to employees not in excluded employment

    B   Form issued when an employee leaves employment

Select which of the following correctly identifies a P60 form.

    C   End of year summary of tax and NICs for all employees for submission to HMRC

    D   End of year summary of tax and NICs per employee to be issued to each employee   LO 2b

---

30   Select which of the following correctly identifies the maximum penalty for filing an incorrect P11D form, where the error was not deliberate.

    A   30% potential lost revenue

    B   70% potential lost revenue

Select which of the following correctly identifies the maximum initial penalty for the late filing of a P11D form.

    C   £300 per return

    D   £3,000 per return   LO 2e

---

31   By which date must an employer provide a completed Form P60 to an employee?

    A   6 July
    B   31 May
    C   19 May
    D   30 April   LO 2d

---

32   Soap Ltd employs 30 people in the manufacture of bathroom products. Remuneration packages offered to employees include company cars and private medical insurance in addition to a competitive basic salary and performance-related bonuses.

Select the date by which Soap Ltd must submit each of the following PAYE returns for 2014/15 to its employees or HMRC to avoid a late filing penalty.

Form P11D

    A   6 July 2015

    B   19 July 2015

Final Full Payment Submission (FPS) for tax year

    C   19 April 2015

    D   19 May 2015

Form P60

    E   19 May 2015

    F   31 May 2015   LO 2d

33 Abacus plc filed its corporation tax return for the year ended 31 December 2013 on time. It has now realised that an error was made and it wishes to rectify this via a claim for 'overpayment relief' as it will otherwise result in an overpayment of tax.

Select which of the following options correctly identifies the latest date by which the claim must be made.

A   31 December 2014
B   31 December 2015
C   31 December 2017
D   31 December 2019   LO 2c

34 Indigo plc filed its corporation tax return for the year ended 31 December 2013 on 30 November 2014. HMRC wishes to correct some obvious errors in the return.

Select which of the following options correctly identifies the latest date by which HMRC may make such corrections.

A   31 August 2015
B   30 September 2015
C   30 November 2015
D   31 December 2015   LO 2c

35 Azure plc filed its corporation tax return for the year ended 31 December 2013 on 28 February 2015. HMRC wishes to conduct an enquiry into the corporation tax return.

Select which of the following options correctly identifies the latest date by which HMRC may give notice of its intention to enquire.

A   31 December 2015
B   28 February 2016
C   31 March 2016
D   30 April 2016   LO 2f

36 Stone plc has no associated companies and taxable total profits of £1,000,000 for its year ended 31 March 2015. It has no dividend income for the year.

Select which of the following options identifies the correct date(s) for the payment of its corporation tax liability for the year ended 31 March 2015.

A   By instalments
B   31 December 2015
C   1 January 2016
D   31 March 2016   LO 2d

37 Ebony plc submitted its corporation tax return for its year ended 31 August 2013 on 1 July 2015. Ebony paid 50% of the corporation tax liability relating to this return on 1 April 2015.

Select which of the following options correctly identifies the maximum fixed penalty for failing to file its corporation tax return on time.

A   £100

B   £1,000

Select which of the following options correctly identifies the maximum possible tax-geared penalty for the **late filing** of its corporation tax return.

C   5% of tax due in the return

D   5% of tax unpaid 6 months after the return was due to be filed   LO 2e

38 Apple Ltd prepares accounts to 30 April each year. Apple Ltd pays corporation tax at the small profits rate.

Year end	Corporation tax due	Date return filed	Date tax paid
30 April 2013	£35,000	12 November 2014	15 December 2014

Select Apple Ltd's maximum liability to penalties for the filing of its corporation tax return for the year ended 30 April 2013.

A   £100 fixed penalty and no tax-geared penalty

B   £100 fixed penalty and 5% tax-geared penalty

C   £1,000 fixed penalty and no tax-geared penalty

D   £1,000 fixed penalty and 5% tax-geared penalty

Select Apple Ltd's liability to penalties for the payment of its corporation tax for the year ended 30 April 2013.

E   5% of tax outstanding

F   10% of tax outstanding

G   15% of tax outstanding

LO 2e

39 Blunt Ltd manufactures stationery and has prepared its corporation tax return for the year ended 31 March 2015.

Jim is a sole trader. He has been a retailer of stationery for many years and has just finished preparing his accounts to 31 December 2014.

Select the latest date for which Blunt Ltd and Jim must keep their business records for tax purposes.

Blunt Ltd

A   31 Mar 2016

B   31 Mar 2020

C   31 Mar 2021

Jim

D   31 Jan 2016

E   31 Jan 2021

F   31 Jan 2022

LO 2a

40 Bone Ltd started to trade on 1 October 2012. Bone Ltd had taxable total profits of £1,600,000 for its first year ended 30 September 2013 and £1,800,000 for its second year ended 30 September 2014. The company received no franked investment income during either period.

State the due date for payment of the corporation tax for each accounting period.

Payment date for year ended 30 September 2013

A   By 1 July 2014

B   By 30 Sep 2014

C   By instalments

Payment date for year ended 30 September 2014

D   By 1 July 2015

E   By 30 Sep 2015

F   By instalments

LO 2d

41 Edmund is a trader whose taxable supplies exceeded the VAT registration threshold ten months ago. His friend explains to him that he should have registered for VAT. Edmund registers and pays the outstanding tax immediately.

Select which of the following options correctly identifies the minimum penalty HMRC could impose for Edmund's late registration.

A   30% of potential lost revenue
B   20% of potential lost revenue
C   10% of potential lost revenue
D   Nil   LO 2e

42 Identify which **two** of the following statements are correct.

A   Amy's VAT return for the quarter to 28 February 2015 should have been submitted by 30 March 2015.

B   Bob & Charles' partnership income tax return for 2014/15 received on 3 November 2015 should be submitted online by 31 January 2016.

C   Daniel's full income tax return for 2014/15 received on 4 July 2015 should be submitted to HMRC by 31 October 2015, if Daniel wants HMRC to calculate the tax.

D   Eagle Ltd's corporation tax return for the year ended 31 December 2014 should be submitted by 1 October 2015.

E   Frank Ltd's P11Ds for 2014/15 should be submitted to HMRC by 6 July 2015.   LO 2d

43 Talia submitted her VAT return for the quarter to 31 December 2014 online on 16 February 2015 and paid the VAT due of £1,280 on that day. She had previously paid VAT late and was subject to a penalty at 2% in her quarter to 30 September 2014.

Talia's penalty for the late payment of VAT for the quarter to 31 December 2014 is

A   £0
B   £25.60
C   £51.20
D   £38.40   LO 2e

44 Rand submitted his VAT return for the quarter to 31 October 2014 online on 15 December 2014 and paid the VAT due of £5,000 on that day. The only other time that he has ever submitted a VAT return late was in his quarter to 30 April 2014.

HMRC is likely to impose a penalty for the late filing of the return for the quarter to 31 October 2014 on Rand of

A   £0

B   £100

C   £200

D   £300   LO 2e

45 Karli set up her business on 1 January 2013. Due to the amount of work she undertook she should have been VAT registered from 30 June 2014 but she did not notify HMRC until 16 November 2015. The unpaid VAT between 30 June 2014 and 16 November 2015 was £10,800. HMRC does not consider being too busy a reasonable excuse for failure to register on time.

The minimum penalty payable by Karli (assuming HMRC deems the failure to notify not to be deliberate) for late registration is

A   Nil
B   £1,080
C   £2,160
D   £3,240

LO 2e

46 John, a sole trader, completed a VAT return for the quarter to 31 December 2013 showing output tax of £120,000 and input tax of £70,000.

In June 2014 John's accountant discovered that the input tax on the VAT return had been overstated by £45,000. This was the first error that John had made on his VAT returns. HMRC was notified and the outstanding tax paid.

Which of the following statements correctly describes the error?

A   Careless

B   Deliberate but not concealed

C   Deliberate and concealed

Which of the following describes the minimum penalty HMRC could charge John for the error?

D   30% of potential lost revenue

E   15% of potential lost revenue

F   0% of potential lost revenue

LO 2e

47 Glitch plc's VAT returns have always been accurate, but the return to 31 December 2014 contains an error. Turnover is correctly stated at £5.6 million, but input tax is overstated by £52,700.

Select which of the following statement is correct.

A   A correction can be made in the next VAT return because the error is less than 1% of turnover
B   A correction cannot be made in the next VAT return because the error exceeds £2,000
C   A correction cannot be made in the next VAT return because the error exceeds £10,000
D   A correction cannot be made in the next VAT return because the error exceeds £50,000 LO 6e

48 Ethel submitted her 2014/15 tax return on 1 December 2015. She omitted to include rental income of £15,000 as she did not think that HMRC would find out about the income. Ethel is a higher rate taxpayer.

HMRC conducts an enquiry into Ethel's return and in reply Ethel makes a disclosure of the rental income.

Which of the following is the minimum penalty that could be charged by HMRC on Ethel for her error?

A   £6,000
B   £4,200
C   £2,100
D   £1,200

LO 2e

49   Which of the following would not constitute a reasonable excuse for late filing of a return?

   A   Serious illness leading up to the filing date
   B   Postal disruption
   C   Failure of a taxpayer's IT systems close to the filing date
   D   Insufficient funds to pay the tax due   LO 2e

50   Shed Ltd has failed to pay its PAYE due of £4,600 for the month ended 5 February 2015 on time.
      Payment was made on 17 March 2015. It had also failed to pay PAYE on time on two other
      occasions during 2014/15.

      What is the amount of any penalty payable by Shed Ltd for late payment of PAYE for the month
      ended 5 February 2015?

   A   £92
   B   Nil
   C   £138
   D   £46   LO 2e

51   A taxpayer may be able to appeal against an information notice

   A   True

   B   False

      A taxpayer may be able to appeal against an inspection notice

   C   True

   D   False   LO 2e

Principles of Taxation: Question Bank

Answer Bank

1   B   Professional intellect

The five fundamental principles of the IESBA Code of Ethics are:

- Integrity
- Objectivity
- Professional competence and due care
- Confidentiality
- Professional behaviour

2   E   Intimidation threat

William is experiencing intimidation threats which occur when a professional accountant is deterred from acting objectively by threats, actual or perceived.

3   A   Self-interest threat; and

D   Familiarity threat

Roger is experiencing familiarity threats which occur when, because of a close relationship, a professional accountant becomes too sympathetic to the interests of others. As Jennifer's husband, he is himself also financially involved, which poses a self-interest threat.

4   C   (i) and (iii) only

Freddy is laundering money through his business and as Florence is aware of this she is required to disclose it to the proper authorities.

Florence should not discuss her decision to go to the authorities with Freddy. This would amount to tipping off which is in itself an offence under money laundering legislation.

Florence may be guilty of money laundering offences as she has assisted Freddy in concealing the proceeds of crime. This carries a prison sentence of up to 14 years.

Florence may well have felt justified in increasing her fee for such risky work but in the circumstances this probably amounts to possessing the proceeds of a criminal activity which is another offence.

5   B   Now

D   The firm's Money Laundering Reporting Officer

Iqmal's responsibility is only to report to the MLRO. If he has reasonable suspicion, he should not try to obtain proof before reporting.

6   B   (i) to (iii) only

An innocent error in a tax return, unlike a deliberate error, would not give rise to proceeds of crime. Tax avoidance is not a crime and so cannot give rise to the proceeds of crime.

7   C   Timescale involved

The other three are explicitly stated in the ICAEW Code as factors to consider.

8   A   Offence committed by Steven

C   Offence committed by Trevor

Steven has committed an offence under the legislation as he has acquired criminal property, the criminal property being the proceeds of tax evasion.

Trevor has committed the offence of tipping off as he is aware that a suspicious activity report (SAR) may have been made by his firm's MLRO.

9   C   Advocacy threat

10 B The relationship that her firm has with the client

  The other three are explicitly stated in the ICAEW Code as factors to consider.

11 A If the threat cannot be sufficiently reduced, the only acceptable level course of action offered is to cease to act.

12 C This is an example of legitimate tax planning so is tax avoidance. The others are all examples of tax evasion.

Chapter 2: Introduction to taxation

1   B   HMRC statements of practice

The annual Finance Act is an Act of Parliament and is therefore a source of law. Case law generally sets a precedent which must be followed unless overruled on appeal or superseded by legislation. Statutory instruments are a form of delegated legislation which are a form of law. Statements of practice are merely a statement of HMRC's interpretation of the law.

2   A   Progressive taxation

   C   Direct tax

A system whereby the overall proportion of taxation increases as income rises is known as a progressive system. Originally income tax represented 15% of Pauline's income. After her pay rise it had risen to 20%.

National insurance contributions are a form of direct taxation.

3   C   Unit principle

This is an example of a unit tax as opposed to VAT which is a value based tax. A unit tax is levied at a flat rate per item regardless of value. It cannot be considered a neutral tax as only supermarkets have to charge it.

4   B   Statutory instruments

While the Budget forms the basis for the Finance Act each year, it is not in itself a form of legislation. Statutory instruments are the biggest single source of tax law each year. Extra-statutory concessions, as their name implies, are not statutory documents. Neither are statements of practice.

5   C   (i), (iii), (iv) and (v) only

As an employee Diana will be liable to income tax and national insurance contributions. As an individual Diana could pay capital gains tax on the disposal of an asset. As an individual Diana must incur VAT in her day to day life as the final consumer. As an individual Diana cannot personally pay corporation tax.

6   C   (i), (ii) and (iv) only

Collect and administer direct taxes

Collect and administer indirect taxes

Collect repayments of student loans

This question is from the sample paper issued by the ICAEW.

1   C   £24,064

    £24,064 only includes Direct Saver Account interest. NISA interest and income tax repayment interest are exempt from income tax.

2   His personal allowance for 2014/15 is £ | 10,260 |

Patrick is born before 6 April 1938.

	£
Personal age allowance	10,660
Less (£27,800 – £27,000) = £800 × $^1/_2$	(400)
Reduced personal age allowance	10,260

3   What is Mackenzie's total income for tax liability for 2014/15? £ | 5,133 |

	Non-savings income £	Savings income £	Total £
Trading profits	35,565		
Bank interest		100	
Net income	35,565	100	35,665
Less personal allowance	(10,000)		(10,000)
Taxable income	25,565	100	25,665

	£
Tax on non-savings income £25,565 × 20%	5,113
Tax on savings income £100 × 20%	20
Income tax liability	5,133

4   The married couple's allowance due to the couple for 2014/15 will initially be given to

    B   Grainne (as Grainne has the higher net income)

The allowance due to the couple to give relief at 10% is

    C   £8,165 (available based on the age of the elder spouse)

5   A   £478

	Non-savings income £	Dividend income £	Total £
Employment earnings	43,915		
Dividend (£1,080 × 100/90)		1,200	
Net income	43,915	1,200	45,115
Less personal allowance	(10,000)		(10,000)
Taxable income	33,915	1,200	35,115

Extend BRB by Gift Aid = £31,865 + (£720 × 100/80) = £32,765

			£
Tax on non-savings income			
£32,765	×	20%	6,553
£1,150	×	40%	460
Tax on dividend income			
£1,200	×	32.5%	390
£35,115			7,403
Less: tax already paid			
Dividend tax credit			(120)
PAYE			(6,805)
Tax payable			478

6   B   £9,250

Only include tips from customers

7   C   £10,450

Paloma was born between 6 April 1938 and 5 April 1948.

	£
Personal age allowance	10,500
Less (£27,100 – £27,000) = £100 × ½	(50)
Reduced personal age allowance	10,450

8   B   £748

£8,165 (MCA available as one spouse is at least 80 by 5 April 2015) × 11/12 (restricted for complete tax months prior to marriage) × 10%

9   B   £80 of National Savings Certificate interest

     E   £40 of dividends received on Y plc shares held in a stocks and shares NISA

10   What is Glenn's total income tax liability for 2014/15? £ | 5,788 |

	Non-savings income £	Dividend income £	Total £
Employment income	38,790		
Dividends £270 × $^{100}/_{90}$		300	
Net income	38,790	300	39,090
Less personal allowance	(10,000)		(10,000)
Taxable income	28,790	300	29,090

	£
Tax on non-savings income £28,790 × 20%	5,758
Tax on dividend income £300 × 10%	30
Income tax liability	5,788

11   C   £20,411

	Non-savings income £	Savings income £	Dividend income £	Total £
Employment earnings	29,351			
Dividends £(540 × 100/90)			600	
Bank interest £(368 × 100/80)		460		
Net income	29,351	460	600	30,411
Less personal allowance	(10,000)			(10,000)
Taxable income	19,351	460	600	20,411

Gift Aid does not affect the calculation of taxable income.

12   Mabel's income tax liability for 2014/15 is £ | 8,675 |

Taxable income (all savings)	£39,000
Tax	£
£2,880 × 10%	288
£28,985 × 20%	5,797
£1,320 (£1,056 × $^{100}/_{80}$) × 20% (extended band)	264
£5,815 × 40%	2,326
£39,000	
Income tax liability	8,675

13   B   He receives basic rate tax relief = At source by paying net of basic rate income tax

     F   He receives higher rate tax relief = By extending the basic rate band

14   What is Gabriella's taxable income for 2014/15? £ | 28,545 |

	Non-savings income £	Savings income £	Dividend income £	Total £
Trading profits	37,145			
Building society interest £480 × $^{100}/_{80}$		600		
Dividends £720 × $^{100}/_{90}$			800	
Net income	37,145	600	800	38,545
Less personal allowance	(10,000)			(10,000)
Taxable income	27,145	600	800	28,545

Premium bond winnings are exempt.

15   B   £10,350

	£
Personal age allowance (born between 6/4/38 and 5/4/48)	10,500
Less abatement	
$^{1}/_{2}$ × (£27,300 – £27,000)	(150)
Reduced personal age allowance	10,350

16   C   £10,140

	£
Personal age allowance (born before 6/4/38)	10,660
Less abatement	
$^{1}/_{2}$ × (£28,040 – £27,000)	(520)
Reduced personal age allowance	10,140

17 C £70

	Non-savings income £	Dividend income £	Total £
Trading profits	41,535		
Dividends £360 × $^{100}/_{90}$		400	
Net income	41,535	400	41,935
Less personal allowance	(10,000)		(10,000)
Taxable income	31,535	400	31,935

Dividend income is the top slice of income hence £31,935 – £31,865 = £70

18 C In 2014/15 the Gift Aid payment will have no impact on Maalik's income tax liability.

Maalik is a basic rate taxpayer in 2014/15 so increasing the upper limit of his basic rate band will have no impact on the calculation of his income tax liability.

19 Bussola's income tax liability is £ [8,384]

	Non-savings income £	Savings income £	Total £
Trading profits	10,810		
Savings income (£29,280 × $^{100}/_{80}$)		36,600	
Net income	10,810	36,600	47,410
Less personal allowance	(10,000)		(10,000)
Taxable income	810	36,600	37,410

	£		£
Tax on non-savings income	810	× 20%	162
Tax on saving income:			
– in starting rate band	2,070	× 10%	207
	2,880		
– in basic rate band	28,985	× 20%	5,797
	31,865		
– in higher rate band	5,545	× 40%	2,218
	37,410		
Income tax liability			8,384

20 What is Chloe's net income for 2014/15? £ [23,190]

	Non-savings income £	Savings income £	Dividend income £	Total £
Trading profits	22,600			
NS&I Investment interest (gross)		190		
Dividend income (£360 × $^{100}/_{90}$)			400	
Net income	22,600	190	400	23,190

NS&I interest is received gross

Interest on NISAs is exempt

21 What is Manav's income tax liability for 2014/15? £ | 3,563 |

	Non-savings income £
Employment income	27,335
Property income	480
Net income	27,815
Less: Personal allowance	(10,000)
Taxable income	17,815

Tax	£
£17,815 × 20%	3,563
Income tax liability	3,563

Income tax repayment interest is exempt.

22 A   Income tax repayment interest

    C   National Lottery winnings

This question is from the sample paper issued by the ICAEW.

23 What is Fredericks's taxable income for 2014/15? £ | 15,815 |

	£
Salary	25,815
Less: Personal allowance	(10,000)
Taxable income	15,815

This question is from the sample paper issued by the ICAEW.

24 What is Frederick's income tax payable under self assessment for 2014/15? £ | 63 |

Taxable income	£15,815

	£
20% on £15,815	3,163
Less: PAYE	(3,100)
Income tax payable	63

This question is from the sample paper issued by the ICAEW.

25 A   Allocated to Bertha as she has the higher net income

This question is from the sample paper issued by the ICAEW.

26 What is Darcy's personal allowance for 2014/15? £ | Nil |

The personal allowance will be nil for any additional rate taxpayer.

27   D   £64,022

		£
Employment income		133,000
Bank interest (£22,080 × 100/80)		27,600
Dividends (£13,500 × 100/90)		15,000
Taxable income		175,600

	£
£31,865 × 20%	6,373
£101,135 × 40%	40,454
£133,000	
£17,000 × 40%	6,800
£150,000	
£10,600 × 45%	4,770
£15,000 × 37.5%	5,625
£175,600	
Income tax liability	64,022

28   What is Josephine's taxable income for 2014/15? £ | 161,000 |

	£
Trading income	125,000
Dividends (£32,400 × 100/90)	36,000
	161,000
Personal allowance	(Nil)
Taxable income	161,000

1   A   606L

	£
Personal allowance	10,000
Less taxable benefits	(2,708)
Less underpaid tax £246 × 100/20	(1,230)
	6,062
PAYE code	606L

2   A   680P

	£
Personal age allowance	10,500
Less underpaid tax £740 × 100/20	(3,700)
	6,800
PAYE code	680P

3   PAYE code ☐ K604

	£
Personal allowance	10,000
Less taxable benefits	(16,050)
Net allowances	(6,050)

Deduct the last digit (gives 605) and deduct 1.

PAYE code	K604

4   A   K126

	£
Personal allowance	10,000
Less taxable benefit	(11,275)
Net allowances	(1,275)

Deduct the last digit (gives 127) and deduct 1.

Hence the code is K126.

5   Jacob's PAYE code for 2014/15 is ☐ 694 ☐ L

	£
Personal allowance	10,000
Less taxable benefit	(3,060)
Net allowances	6,940

Deduct the last digit and add L

6   B   742L

	£
Personal allowance	10,000
Less deduction (£1,032 × 100/40)	(2,580)
Net allowances	7,420

Deduct the last digit and add L.

7   The taxable benefits assessable on Harry in 2014/15 are £ $\boxed{14,944}$

$$\frac{180-95}{5} = 17$$

Percentage = 12 + 17 + 3 (diesel) = 32%

Car benefit = 32% × 25,000 = £8,000

Fuel benefit = 32% × 21,700 = £6,944

8   The additional employment income for each of the company's employees in 2014/15 as a result of the provision of the two benefits is £ $\boxed{720}$

Telephone = £0

Childcare = £(70 – 55) × 48 weeks = £720

9   Private health insurance, costing Bony Ltd £800. The same insurance would have cost Jacob £1,100.

A   £800

PHI = £800 as cost to employer

A television out of stock which cost £200 to manufacture but would cost Bony Ltd £800 to buy in from another supplier.

C   £200

Television = £200 as marginal cost to employer

A car parking space at a car park near to the office which cost Bony Ltd £500 in 2014/15.

E   £0

Car parking space = Nil as exempt

10   C   £2,833

£3,090 × 11/12 = £2,833 = Pro rated van benefit

11   B   £250

For non P11D employees (ie employees earning less than £8,500 per the emoluments test), benefits in the form of assets are taxable at the amount for which they can be exchanged into cash (second hand value).

12   A   £0

No benefit for cycle equipment made available to all employees.

No benefit for childcare vouchers of less than or equal to £55 per week for those in the scheme prior to 6 April 2011. For those joining the scheme on or after 6 April 2011 there is no benefit for childcare vouchers of less than or equal to £55 per week for a basic rate taxpayer or £28 per week for a higher rate taxpayer. In all cases they must be for use with approved childcare providers.

13   The 'cost' of the flat for the purpose of computing the additional yearly rental benefit for 2014/15 is £ $\boxed{327,000}$

£327,000 = original cost plus enhancement pre 2014/15

= £(310,000 + 17,000)

Market value is only relevant if owned for six years prior to first use. The double glazing is not included because it was not installed before the start of this tax year, however it will be used to calculate the benefit in 2015/16.

14 The taxable benefit assessable on Amy in 2014/15 is £ [8,444]

$$\frac{170 - 95}{5} = 15$$

Percentage = 12 + 15 = 27%

Car benefit = 27% × 20,000 × 9/12 = £4,050

Fuel benefit = 27% × 21,700 × 9/12 = £4,394

15 B £3,713

$$\frac{185 - 95}{5} = 18$$

Percentage = 12 + 18 + 3 (diesel) = 33%

Car benefit = 33% × 15,000 = £4,950 × 9/12 = £3,713

16 The benefit assessable on Pirro in respect of the computer is £ [zero]

As the private use of the computer is insignificant (< 40%) there will be no assessable benefit.

17 Pippin is provided with a van with CO_2 emissions of 190 g/km, by his employer Joker Ltd. Joker Ltd pay for all petrol for the van. Pippin has an assessable fuel benefit based on the CO_2 emissions.

B   Incorrect – the fuel benefit on a company van is £581 per annum irrespective of emissions.

Piers makes a nominal contribution towards the fuel cost on his company car of £10 per month. This accounts for about 95% of his private use. He is able to reduce his fuel benefit by £120 pa.

D   Incorrect – a contribution towards private fuel only reduces the benefit if it is a 100% contribution (reducing the benefit to NIL)

18 The taxable benefit of the flat in 2014/15 is £ [24,600]

	£
Annual value	8,675
Additional yearly rental benefit £(565,000 – 75,000) × 3.25%	15,925
Taxable benefit	24,600

19 C £30

No benefit for the canteen as it is made available to all employees.

As the overnight expenses exceed £5 per night the whole amount becomes chargeable.

20 A £52,500

Jacob's employment income for the year is the amount actually received in the tax year, ie his salary of £36,000 plus the bonus of £16,500 received on 30 April 2014.

21 B Employees in excluded employment are taxed on benefits which can be converted into cash. The assessable amount is the marginal cost to the employer. False.

Employees in excluded employment are taxed on benefits which can be sold. However, the assessable amount is based on their second hand value. Employees not in excluded employment are assessed on the marginal cost of providing an asset where no specific rule exists as to how the value of that asset should be quantified.

C   Employees in excluded employment are sometimes called 'P9D' employees. True.

Employees in excluded employment are often referred to as P9D employees. Employees not in excluded employment are often referred to as P11D employees.

22 C £8,000

The taxable benefit is the higher of the annual rateable value and the rent paid by the employer (if any) less any contribution by the employee:

	£
Higher of rent/rateable value	15,000
Less employee contribution	(7,000)
Taxable benefit	8,000

23 B 1 and 2 only

Accommodation is not job related simply because it enables the employee to work longer hours by reducing time spent commuting. Accommodation provided to directors owning more than 5% of the company is only job related if it is provided for reasons of security.

24 A £18,000

The taxable benefit of expensive living accommodation is calculated in two parts. Where accommodation is provided more than six years after its acquisition and its original cost plus improvements as at first occupation exceeds £75,000 market value is used instead of original cost. In this case Sally first occupies the property more than six years after its acquisition. However its original cost plus improvements is only £60,000. Thus the property does not qualify as expensive accommodation (despite its current market value) and Sally is only taxable on the annual rateable value.

25 C £22,450

The taxable benefit for expensive accommodation is the annual rateable value plus: ((original cost less £75,000) × official rate of interest). The taxable benefit then needs to be prorated for the actual period of use in the tax year, ie 6 August 2014 – 5 April 2015 for 2014/15:

[£21,000 + ((£465,000 – £75,000) × 3.25%)] × 8/12 = £22,450

26 A £4,147

The benefit is calculated as follows.

	£
Annual rateable value	19,000
Less: contribution by employee	(12,000)
	7,000
Additional yearly rent	
(£325,000 + £45,000 – £75,000) × 3.25%	9,588
Total benefit	16,588
Pro rate for actual occupation in the year × 3/12	4,147

Note that the additional yearly rent is based on the original cost plus capital improvements made before the start of the tax year in which the benefit is charged, ie prior to 6 April 2014 in this case.

27 A £4,755

The taxable benefit for the petrol company car is:

$$\frac{110 - 95}{5} = 3$$

Percentage = 12 + 3 = 15%

Car benefit = 15% × £10,000 = £1,500

Fuel benefit = 15% × £21,700 = £3,255

Where private fuel is only partly repaid by the employer no reduction is given to the taxable benefit. Either the private fuel benefit is fully reimbursed by the employee or the full £21,100 at the appropriate percentage is taxable on the employee.

28   B   £4,020

The taxable benefit for the diesel company car, which has CO_2 emissions exceeding 75g/km but less than 95g/km, is:

11% + 3% (diesel) = 14%

14% × £33,000 (car list price) - £600 (employee contribution) = £4,020

The original list price is used to compute the taxable benefit.

29   B   £3,671

The taxable benefit for a company van with private use is £3,090. The van fuel benefit is £581. Private use of vans does not include home to work.

30   D   £50

As Jasper is in excluded employment (earnings + benefits as if were not in excluded employment <£8,500) there is no benefit in respect of the van.

Any assets which can be converted into cash, ie sold, are assessed based on their second hand value. The benefit of the gift of video equipment is therefore just £50.

31   C   £1,200

Childcare vouchers of up to £55 per week are exempt as Robert was in the scheme prior to 6 April 2011 (otherwise only £28 per week would be exempt as he is a higher rate taxpayer). Meal vouchers are taxable in full.

32   D   £0

Non-cash gifts from a third party of up to £250 per tax year from the same donor are exempt.

Where an employee not in excluded employment receives a benefit for which there is no specific rule under the benefits code, the benefit should be assessed based on the marginal cost to the employer. Given that the plane would operate with or without Alexandra on board and there were always spare seats available, the marginal cost to her employer of Alexandra's travel is £Nil. Her total taxable benefit is therefore £Nil.

33   D   £0

Long service awards are exempt where minimum service is 20 years and are not in cash and equate to less than £50 per year of service.

Subsidies to public bus services with free travel for employees in return, are exempt.

Hettie's taxable benefits are therefore £Nil.

34   B   Employer contributions – Exempt

     D   Childcare vouchers – Exempt

     E   Living accommodation – Taxable

This question is from the sample paper issued by the ICAEW.

35   In calculating Charlie's total employment income for 2014/15, the amount which will be included for the car benefit is £ [3,780]

160 – 95 = 65g/km

65 ÷ 5 = 13%

Taxable percentage 28% (12% + 13% + 3% diesel)

£18,000 × 9/12 × 28% = £3,780

The benefit is time apportioned as the car was available from 1 July 2014

This question is from the sample paper issued by the ICAEW.

36   C   The car has emissions not exceeding 75g/km so the percentage used is 5%.

As it is a diesel car this must then be increased by 3% to 8%.

£16,000 × 8% = £1,280

1   A   Amy has just sold a house that she bought three months ago. She has spent £40,000 to make the property more attractive to potential purchasers. Amy has not lived in this house.

    D   Dante has an interest in vintage cars. He has just sold a car that he has been renovating for the last six months. This is the seventh renovated car that he has sold in the last two years.

2   B   Provision of own equipment

    E   Correction of own work

3   A case of wine costing £48 to a customer. Each bottle had the name of the garage on the label.

    B   Disallowable

    Gifts to customers of alcohol

    Four bottles of spirits costing £90 to an employee.

    C   Allowable

    Gifts to employee are allowable as part of staff costs (but benefit on employee)

    Cash of £60 to each of his three junior employees.

    E   Allowable

    Cash bonus to employee is simply remuneration, ie part of staff costs (but taxable on employee)

4   The hire charge allowable as a deduction against trading profits is £ | 4,000 |

    £5,000 × 80% (private use)

    There is no flat rate disallowance as CO_2 emissions do not exceed 130g/km.

5   B   Legal fees of a successful appeal against a tax assessment

    E   Cost of taking out a new five-year lease on business premises

6   Expenditure shown in the profit and loss account is not always allowable for tax purposes. Disallowable expenditure must be added back when computing the taxable trading profits.

    A   Correct – the profit in the P&L account has been reduced by this amount therefore it should be added back.

    The building that you are acquiring is dilapidated and requires repair work. You are not able to use the building until this work has been completed. The additional expenditure incurred on this repair work is allowable when computing taxable trading profits.

    D   Incorrect – the expenditure on the second hand asset makes it fit for purpose, so is capital expenditure and is not allowable.

7   A   A gift of a £10 bottle of wine to each of 200 potential new customers as a marketing method to entice them to buy more wine in the future, ie a trade sample.

    B   Gifts to his two employees of a wine hamper costing him £60 for each employee.

    A sample of trading stock to potential customers is allowable – it is irrelevant that it is alcohol.

    Gifts to employees are allowable.

    The legal fees on a **new** short lease are disallowable.

    Donations to national charities are disallowable.

8   A   Costs of registering a patent for trade use.

     D   The legal costs for renewing the ten-year lease on his shop premises.

          Costs of registering a patent for trade use are specifically allowable.

          Fees for **renewal** of a short lease are allowable.

          Parking fines incurred by a sole trader are always disallowable.

          The payment to his wife is only partly allowable.

9   D   (i) only

          Only gifts to local charities are allowable .

10   A   The number of transactions

     C   Changes to the asset

          Re: Interval of time between purchase and sale – a **short** length of ownership would indicate trade.

          Re: correction of own work – this is not one of the badges of trade.

11   A   £2,400

          Repairs to a newly acquired second hand asset are not allowable if the repair is required in order to make it fit for purpose.

          Roof repairs and redecorating are maintenance in order to take an asset back to its original condition hence allowable.

12   D   £11,320

          Only a reasonable payment to a family member is allowable, so add back Peter's excess salary of £11,000 (£14,000 – £3,000)

          The private proportion of Marion's motor expenses is not allowable 40% × £800 = £320

13   A   Add back £300

	£
The write off of the former employee loan needs to be added back	500
The recovery of the former employee loan must be deducted	(200)
Net effect	300

          The write off of trade debts is allowable, as is the movement on specific provisions.

14   B   £4,300

          The flight must be added back as it is not wholly and exclusively for business purposes (duality).

          Entertaining of customers must always be disallowed ie added back.

          The staff entertaining is allowable for the business as long as it is reasonable (the individuals will however have a taxable benefit for employment income purposes as it exceeds the limit permitted for employment income purposes of £150 pa).

15   A   £490

          Fines of the proprietor are merely an appropriation of profits and disallowed.

          Gifts out of stock to a UK educational establishment are specifically allowable.

          Trade subscriptions are allowable.

16 C £470

Fines or interest relating to tax are specifically disallowed for individuals so £270 is disallowed.

The renewal costs of a short lease are allowable.

The employer's pension contributions are allowable in the year actually paid so £200 is disallowed.

17 B £428 added back

The amount to be added back/disallowed is 15% × £3,800 × 9/12 = £428

There is a 15% disallowance as the car has CO_2 emissions that exceed 130g/km.

18 B Restaurant bill – do not adjust

D Staff costs – do not adjust

19 A An amount of £938 must be added back   – True

D The basic rate band must be extended by £938   – False

The basic rate band must be extended by the gross amount of £1,173 (£938 × 100/80)

20 The amount by which accounting profits need to be increased to arrive at trading profits, in relation to the shoes is £ [450]

As no adjustment has been made in the accounts the profits must be increased by the full retail price.

If the accounts had already been adjusted for the cost element then the only adjustment required would be for the profit of £230 (£450 – £220).

21 D £29,843

The disallowable elements to be added back are those relating directly to Sam (ie his drawings).

	£
Sam's salary	27,000
Class 2 contributions (for Sam)	143
Sam's pension contributions	2,700
	29,843

22 The amount to be added back in calculating the tax adjusted profits is £ [2,300]

There are two amounts that are specifically disallowed by legislation:

	£
Legal fees on the preparation of the partnership agreement	800
Legal fees relating to a new 10 year lease on the office premises	1,500
	2,300

23 A A bill from a hotel for £480 (including VAT of £80) for a meal   – Add back £480

E A bill from a hotel for £5,000 (excluding VAT) for the annual staff party   – Do not adjust

Entertaining customers is disallowable expenditure but entertaining staff is allowable. Furthermore irrecoverable VAT (on UK client entertaining) is allowable only if the expenditure to which it relates is allowable. As the client entertaining is disallowable the VAT on this is also disallowable.

24 A Bank interest received of £280 on the business bank account   – Deduct £280

E Profit of £490 on disposal of a machine   – Deduct £490

Both of these amounts have increased accounting profit but neither are trading income, so a deduction must be made for each one.

25 B £720

The disallowable amounts to be added back are

	£
Relating to James' car (30% × £2,000)	600
Relating to the sales manager's car – all allowable	–
Hire purchase interest payable on James' car (30% × £400)	120
	720

26 B Caroline has personally paid for her home telephone bills – Reduce trading profits by £300

E Caroline made a £200 donation to a local hospice – Reduce trading profits by £200

27 B £10,000 of salary to her husband who works as a bookkeeper – Do not adjust

C Irrecoverable VAT of £3,500 on a company car purchased for an employee – Adjust

As Soria's husband is being paid a reasonable salary for the work done no adjustment is required.

VAT cannot be recovered on motor cars as the VAT legislation forbids this recovery. Irrecoverable VAT is added to the overall cost of the car for the business. As the purchase of a car is capital expenditure it is disallowable and the VAT on this is also disallowable. The VAT should be included as part of the cost of the car in the capital allowances computation.

28 B £1,234

Specific bad debts written off are an allowable deduction.

Interest on late payment of income tax is a disallowable expense.

1   B   The maximum capital allowances that Nina will receive in respect of the purchase of the photocopier in the year ended 30 April 2015 are £2,070

£2,300 × 90% = £2,070

      F   The maximum capital allowances that Nina will receive in respect of the purchase of the car in the year ended 30 April 2015 are £373

18% × £2,300 × 90% = £373

2   A   The maximum capital allowances that Aasia will receive in respect of the purchase of the photocopier in the period ended 31 March 2015 are £3,000 as it is covered by the AIA (prorated to £500,000 × 10/12 = £416,667).

      F   The maximum capital allowances that Aasia will receive in respect of the purchase of the car in the period ended 31 March 2015 are £450

18% × 10/12 × £3,000 = £450

3   A   The maximum capital allowances available on the computer in the period to 31 January 2015 are £5,000 as it is covered by the AIA (prorated to £500,000 × 4/12 = £166,667).

      F   The maximum capital allowances available on the car in the period to 31 January 2015 are £792

£13,200 × 18% × 4/12 = £792

4   C   The maximum capital allowance claim available to Barbara for the period is £10,560

£13,200 (covered by AIA) × 80% = £10,560

5   B   Expenditure is only allowable for the purposes of computing trading profits if it has been incurred wholly, exclusively and necessarily for the purposes of the trade.

Incorrect

The requirement is wholly & exclusively. The additional requirement of necessarily only applies to expenses allowable for employment income.

      D   Capital expenditure is not allowable in computing trading profits but will always result in capital allowances.

Incorrect

It will **often** result in capital allowances but not always (eg cost of a new office building)

6   B   Capital expenditure is not allowable in computing trading profits but will sometimes result in capital allowances.

      C   Expenditure is only allowable for the purposes of computing trading profits if it has been incurred wholly and exclusively for the purposes of the trade.

7   Murphy's maximum capital allowances for the period ended 5 April 2015 are £ [518,520]

Y/e 5.4.15	FYA £	Main pool £	Allowances £
Acquisitions (FYA):			
1.9.14 Low emission car	16,000		
FYA @ 100%	(16,000)		16,000
	Nil		
Acquisitions (AIA):			
1.7.14 Machinery		514,000	
AIA		(500,000)	500,000
		14,000	
WDA @ 18%		(2,520)	2,520
TWDV c/f		11,480	
Allowances			518,520

8   The partnership's maximum capital allowances for the year ended 31 March 2015 are
£ [3,236]

		£
Murray's car	£17,000 × 18% × 60%	1,836
Nuri's car – balancing allowance (£8,000 – £6,000)		
Balancing allowance	£2,000 × 70% =	1,400
		3,236

9   C   £3,600

       The balancing allowance for full business use is £4,800 (£15,000 – £10,200)

       This is restricted to the business proportion £3,600 (75% × £4,800)

10   Capital allowances £ [20,000]

Y/e 31.5.15	FYA £	Main pool £	Allowances £
Acquisitions (FYA):			
20.3.15 Low emission car	8,000		
FYA @ 100%	(8,000)		8,000
	Nil		
Acquisitions (AIA):			
12.2.15 Computer		10,000	
1.5.15 Office furniture		2,000	
AIA		(12,000)	12,000
TWDV c/f		Nil	
Allowances			20,000

11   Capital allowances   £ [1,458]

1.9.14 – 31.5.15	Car ≤130g/km £		Allowances £
Addition	18,000		
WDA 18% × 9/12	(2,430)	× 60%	1,458
	15,570		

This question is from the sample paper issued by the ICAEW.

12 C   Balancing allowance of £1,750

y/e 31.3.15	Expensive car £		Allowances £
TWDV brought forward	17,000		
Disposal	(14,500)		
Balancing allowance	2,500	× 70%	1,750

13 The maximum amount of capital allowances that can be claimed in the year ended 31 May 2015 relating to this car is £ ⬚ 3,240

The car has a writing down allowance of 18% per annum as it will go in the main pool. This is not restricted for private use by an *employee*.

14 B   £1,440

1.10.14 – 31.3.15 (6 months)	Main pool £	Allowances £
Addition	16,000	
WDA @ 18% × 6/12	(1,440)	1,440
TWDV c/f	14,560	

15 A   £8,560

1.7.14 – 31.3.15 (9 months)	Main pool £	Allowances £
TWDV b/f	560	
Acquisitions (AIA):		
Computer	8,000	
AIA (£500,000 × 9/12 = £375,000)	(8,000)	8,000
	560	
Write-off of small pool (£1,000 × 9/12 = £750)	(560)	560
TWDV c/f	0	
Allowances		8,560

As the small pool is less than the prorated minimum balance of £750, it may be written off in full.

16 The maximum capital allowances that can be claimed by Matthew for the year ended 31 December 2014 are £ ⬚ 342

As the business continues there is no balancing adjustment in the main pool on the disposal of the machine. (Once the pool drops to £1,000 or less in a later year, the whole pool may be written off.)

Y/e 31.12.14	Main pool £	Allowances £
TWDV brought forward	2,300	
Disposal	(400)	
	1,900	
WDA @ 18%	(342)	342
TWDV carried forward	1,558	

17 The maximum capital allowances that can be claimed by Max for the year ended 30 September 2014 are £ ⬚ 3,870

Y/e 30.9.14	Main pool £	Allowances £
TWDV brought forward	25,400	
Disposal (use cost as sale proceeds exceed cost)	(3,900)	
	21,500	
WDA @ 18%	(3,870)	3,870
TWDV carried forward	17,630	

18 C £11,160

1.10.14 – 31.3.15 (6 months)	FYA £	Main pool £	Allowances £
TWDV brought forward		24,000	
WDA @ 18% × 6/12		(2,160)	2,160
Additions (FYA)	9,000		
FYA @ 100% (low emission car)	(9,000)		9,000
TWDV carried forward	Nil	21,840	
Total allowances			11,160

The FYA is not pro-rated for short accounting periods.

19 B £212,208

1.11.14 – 31.3.15 (5 months)	Main pool £	Allowances £
Acquisitions (AIA):		
23.11.14 Machine	260,000	
AIA (£500,000 × 5/12)	(208,333)	208,333
	51,667	
WDA @ 18% × 5/12	(3,875)	3,875
TWDV c/f	47,792	
Allowances		212,208

20 B Car with emission of 125g/km costing £14,000 on 10 June 2014 with 20% private use by one of the employees

21 The maximum capital allowances that can be claimed by Jamie for the year ended 31 January 2015 are £ ⬚ 4,626

Y/e 31.1.15	Main pool £	Allowances £
TWDV brought forward	31,000	
Disposal	(5,300)	
	25,700	
WDA @ 18%	(4,626)	4,626
TWDV c/f	21,074	

22 The maximum capital allowances that can be claimed by Janice on the machine for the year ended 5 April 2015 are £ ⬚ 503,600

Y/e 5.4.15	Main pool £	Allowances £
Acquisitions (AIA):		
1.5.14 Machine	520,000	
AIA	(500,000)	500,000
	20,000	
WDA @ 18%	(3,600)	3,600
TWDV c/f	16,400	
Allowances		503,600

1   The trading profits assessable on Rafael in 2014/15 are £ | 39,300 |

y/e 30 June 2014	Total £	Rafael £	Saeed £	Tadeo £
Salary	10,000		10,000	
Interest	6,100	3,000	1,200	1,900
Balance 1:1:1	108,900	36,300	36,300	36,300
	125,000	39,300	47,500	38,200

Rafael has taxable trading profits of £39,300 for the year ended 30 June 2014. As the partnership is not new this will be taxed on Rafael in 2014/15.

2   A   What is Townshend's trading profit assessment for 2013/14? £38,000

CYB

Basis period y/e 30 April 2013 = £38,000

E   What is Townshend's trading profit assessment for 2014/15? £50,000

Final tax year (2014/15)

	£
Basis period 1 May 2013 to 30 November 2014	
y/e 30 April 2014	34,000
p/e 30 November 2014	23,000
	57,000
Less overlap profits	(7,000)
	50,000

3   B   Jabir £32,958   Kadin £28,292

y/e 31 August 2015	Total £	Jabir £	Kadin £
Salary	8,000	8,000	
PSR 1:1	97,000	48,500	48,500
	105,000	56,500	48,500
2014/15 opening years (7/12)		32,958	28,292

First tax year (2014/15)

Actual basis

Basis period 1 September 2014 to 5 April 2015

4   B   First accounts are 6 months ended 5 April 2015 with future accounts to 5 April

First year 2014/15 = p/e 5 April 2015

Second year 2015/16 = y/e 5 April 2016 etc

5   The trading profits assessable on Cliff in 2014/15 are £ | 49,500 |

y/e 30 September 2014	Total £	Val £	Cliff £	Frank £
Interest on capital (5%)	6,000	2,500	1,500	2,000
PSR 1:1:1	144,000	48,000	48,000	48,000
	150,000	50,500	49,500	50,000

CYB applies as the partnership has traded for many years.

6 B Tom £83,333   Dick £36,667

Y/e 31 Oct 2014	*Total*	*Tom*	*Dick*
	£	£	£
Salary	10,000	10,000	
PSR 2:1	110,000	73,333	36,667
	120,000	83,333	36,667

CYB applies as the partnership has traded for many years.

7 Raanan's trading profit assessment for 2014/15 is £ [7,000]

Final tax year (2014/15)

	£
Basis period 1 February 2014 to 31 December 2014	
P/e 31 December 2014	15,000
Less unrelieved overlap profits	(8,000)
	7,000

Penultimate tax year (2013/14)
CYB
Basis period y/e 31 January 2014

8 C £1,300

First tax year (2012/13)
Actual basis
Basis period 1 January 2013 to 5 April 2013

$3/12 \times £6,000 = £1,500$

Second tax year (2013/14)
12 month period ending in the tax year
Basis period 1 January 2013 to 31 December 2013

Year ended 31 December 2013 = £6,000

Overlap profits

1 January 2013 to 5 April 2013 = £1,500

Final tax year (2014/15)

	£
Basis period 1 January 2014 to 28 February 2015	
P/e 28 February 2015	2,800
Less unrelieved overlap profits	(1,500)
	1,300

9 D £21,000

Final tax year (2014/15)

	£
Basis period 1 October 2013 to 30 April 2014	
P/e 30 April 2014	25,000
Less unrelieved overlap profits	(4,000)
	21,000

Penultimate tax year (2013/14)
Basis period y/e 30 September 2013

10 B £18,000

First tax year (2014/15)
Actual basis
Basis period 1 July 2014 to 5 April 2015 = $9/12 \times £24,000 = £18,000$

11 B £18,000

First tax year (2014/15)
Actual basis
Basis period 1 July 2014 to 5 April 2015

Second tax year (2015/16)
CYB
Basis period y/e 30 June 2015

Overlap profits 1 July 2014 to 5 April 2015 = 9/12 × £24,000 = £18,000

12 B Taxable trading profits for 2013/14 are £5,000

D Taxable trading profits for 2014/15 are £22,500

First tax year (2013/14)
Actual basis
Basis period 1 January 2014 to 5 April 2014
3/6 × £10,000   £5,000

Second tax year (2014/15)
Period of accounts in second tax year is less than 12 months
Basis period 1 January 2014 to 31 December 2014

		£
P/e 30 June 2014		10,000
1 July 2014 to 31 Dec 2014	6/12 × £25,000	12,500
		22,500

13 A £28,000 is taxable in 2014/15, representing the period 6 April 2014 to 5 April 2015.

12/18 × £42,000 – no accounting period ending in second tax year so actual basis applies.

14 The taxable trading profit for 2014/15 is £ [85,000]

First tax year (2014/15)

Actual basis: 1 July 2014 to 5 April 2015 = £60,000 + (3/12 × £100,000)

15 Ray's overlap profits are £ [25,000]

First year actual basis: 1 July 2014 to 5 April 2015 = £60,000 + (3/12 × £100,000)

Second year CYB year ended 31 December 2015 = £100,000

Overlap = 1 January 2015 to 5 April 2015 = 3/12 × £100,000 = £25,000

16 D Amber £145,000   Betty £95,000

	Total £	Amber £	Betty £
6 months to 30 June			
PSR (£120,000) 2:1	120,000	80,000	40,000
6 months to 31 December			
Salary (× 6/12)	10,000	10,000	
PSR (£110,000) 1:1	110,000	55,000	55,000
	240,000	145,000	95,000

17 The trading profits assessable on Aubrey in 2014/15 are £ [50,750]

	Total £	Aubrey £	Elaine £
Y/e 30 September 2014			
Interest on capital (5%)	3,500	2,500	1,000
PSR 1:1	96,500	48,250	48,250
	100,000	50,750	49,250

CYB applies as the partnership has traded for many years.

18   D   £30,000

	Total £	David £	Doreen £
Y/e 30 June 2015 PSR 2:1	120,000	80,000	40,000

First year actual basis (2014/15)

1 July 2014 to 5 April 2015

9/12 × £40,000 = £30,000

19   Florian's taxable trading profit for 2014/15 is £ | 14,820 |

2013/14 = year ended 31 January 2014 = £21,200

2014/15 = remaining profits less overlap = £17,430 – 2,610= £14,820

20   Imogen's assessable trading profits for 2014/15 are £ | 41,680 |

	Main pool £	Allowances £
1.8.14-31.5.15 (10 months) Acquisitions (AIA):		
Office equipment	10,000	
Office shelving	500	
AIA	(10,500)	10,500
(500,000 × 10/12 = 416,667 so all covered by AIA)		
Other acquisitions:		
Car	16,000	
WDA 18% × 10/12	(2,400)	2,400
TWDV c/f	13,600	
Allowances		12,900

10 m/e 31 May 2015	£
Trading profit	65,000
Capital allowances	(12,900)
Tax adjusted trading profit	52,100
2014/15 – 1 August 2014 to 5 April 2015 8/10 × £52,100	41,680

21   Jennifer's trading profit assessment for 2014/15 is £ | 14,124 |

8 m/e 30 June 2015	£
Trading profit	23,520
Capital allowances £7,680 × 18% × 8/12	(922)
Tax adjusted trading profit	22,598
2014/15 – 1 November 2014 to 5 April 2015 5/8 × £22,598	14,124

22   B   £39,990

	Total £	Leroy £	Annabelle £
Interest on capital (5%)	2,900	1,750	1,150
Balance (2:3)	95,600	38,240	57,360
Tax adjusted profits	98,500	39,990	58,510

This question is from the sample paper issued by the ICAEW.

23 B £45,607

2013/14 (1.1.14 to 5.4.14)

2014/15 (1.3.14 to 28.2.15)

Profits 2014/15

$12/14 \times £53,208 = \underline{£45,607}$

This question is from the sample paper issued by the ICAEW.

24 D £33,100

	£	£
Total receipts	63,000	
Less receipt from sale of car as not taxable as trading income	(3,000)	
		60,000
Total payments	27,000	
Less interest paid on bank loan (max £500)	(100)	
		(26,900)
Taxable trading profit		33,100

25 A £24,300

Taxable trading profits for the ten months ended 30 April 2015 are £27,000 (£58,000 – £31,000).

The opening year rules apply. In 2014/15 tax the actual profits from 1 July 2014 to 5 April 2015.

Profits 2014/15

$9/10 \times £27,000 = \underline{£24,300}$

1   A   Class 1 primary

    C   Class 2

        Sho's trading profits are below the annual lower profits limit for Class 4 NIC.

2   B   Wagner Ltd will pay Class 4 NICs on the profits of £80,000. Incorrect

        Companies do not pay Class 4 NIC.

    C   George will pay Class 1 primary NICs on his earnings of £15,000. Correct

        He is below retirement age and his earnings are above the primary threshold.

    F   Wagner Ltd will pay Class 1 secondary NICs on total employee remuneration of £65,000. Incorrect

        Class 1 secondary NICs are not paid on dividends. It will therefore be liable to secondary Class 1 NIC on £20,000 + £15,000 = £35,000.

3   Steven's Class 4 national insurance contributions for 2014/15 are £ | 409 |

	£
Adjusted trading profit before capital allowances	15,000
Less capital allowances	(2,500)
Tax adjusted trading profits for 2013/14	12,500

    Class 4 NICs:
    (£12,500 – £7,956) × 9% = £409

4   B   £3,115

	£
9% (£41,865 – £7,956)	3,052
2% (£45,000 – £41,865)	63
	3,115

5   His total national insurance contributions for 2014/15 are £ | 1,227 |

		£
Class 2	52 × £2.75	143
Class 4	9% (£20,000 – £7,956)	1,084
		1,227

6   The Class 1 secondary contributions payable by Ball Ltd in 2014/15 in respect of Lena are £ | 4,265 |

	£
Class 1 secondary (£38,862 – £7,956) × 13.8%	4,265

    Class 1 secondary contributions are not paid on benefits. Taxable benefits (the car only in this case) give rise to a liability to Class 1A NIC.

7   The Class 1A contributions payable by Ball Ltd in 2014/15 in respect of Lena are £ | 690 |

	£
Class 1A £5,000 × 13.8%	690

    Class 1A contributions are not paid on exempt benefits (car parking space).

8   Boris will have Class 1 primary contributions deducted from his wages.

B   Incorrect

Jinx Ltd must pay Class 1 secondary contributions in relation to Boris's earnings.

C   Correct

When an individual reaches retirement age he stops paying Class 1 primary contributions but his employer must still pay Class 1 secondary contributions.

9   The total national insurance liability of the company for 2014/15 is £ [1,816]

Only liability is to Class 1 secondary NIC (less the £2,000 employment allowance)

(£35,610 – £7,956) × 13.8% = £3,816 - £2,000 = £1,816

10   C   £5,526

		£
Class 1 secondary	(£45,000 – £7,956) × 13.8%	5,112
Class 1 A	£3,000 × 13.8%	414
		5,526

11   B   Capital gains tax – No

C   Income tax – Yes (as miscellaneous income)

F   National insurance – No (miscellaneous income is not earnings)

This question is from the sample paper issued by the ICAEW.

12   C   Adam must register to pay Class 2 NICs as soon as possible after commencing to trade.

13   The total national insurance liability of Belinda for 2014/15 is £ [3,891]

	£
Class 1 primary	
(£3,300 – £663) × 12% = £316 × 11 months	3,476
(£3,489 – £663) × 12% = £339 × 1 month	339
(£7,300 – £3,489) × 2% = £76 × 1 month	76
Total	3,891

ICAEW

1   D   Partners individually

The partnership is not taxable in its own right; rather it is an amalgamation of individuals effectively taxed as sole traders. Neither are partners taxed jointly. Every individual is liable to capital gains tax independently. As the asset is owned by all the partners, each partner must declare his share of any gain on his own self-assessment return.

2   A   15 March 2015

The date of disposal for capital gains purposes is the date on which the contract for disposal becomes unconditional. In this case the contract became unconditional on the date contracts were exchanged. The date legal title passes, physical possession is obtained, or payment is made are all irrelevant.

3   C   Stamp duty land tax paid on the purchase of land may be deducted as part of cost on a subsequent disposal of the land.

Assets which are inherited are treated as being acquired by the donee at their probate value ie at their value at the time of the donor's death. This is sometimes known as the tax-free uplift on death.

Wasting chattels are always exempt from CGT. The £6,000 rule applies to non-wasting chattels.

Where an asset is not sold at arm's length the proceeds are deemed to be market value at the time of sale or gift.

4   A   £(7,800)

As a non-wasting asset, the chattel rules apply. As it was sold at a loss, actual proceeds are substituted by deemed proceeds of £6,000 to restrict the loss.

	£
Deemed proceeds	6,000
Less auctioneer's fees	(800)
Net sale proceeds	5,200
Less cost	(13,000)
Loss	(7,800)

5   B   Gain of £4,500 on the disposal of a caravan – exempt

     D   Gain of £1,000 on the sale of a sculpture. The sculpture originally cost £4,000 – exempt

The caravan is a wasting asset which is an exempt asset.

The sculpture is a non-wasting chattel, which is a chargeable asset. However, as it was both bought and sold for less than £6,000, it is specifically exempt.

6   D   £8,090

The chair is a non-wasting asset and is liable to capital gains tax subject to the chattel rules. As it was purchased for less than £6,000 and sold for more than £6,000 there is a marginal gain. The gain is the lower of the actual gain and $5/3 \times$ (Gross proceeds – £6,000):

Actual gain = £11,150 – £560 – £2,500 = £8,090

$5/3 \times$ (£11,150 – £6,000) = £8,583

7   C   His unused annual exempt amount from 2013/14 – no effect

    E   Becoming a higher-rate tax payer for the first time – increase capital gains tax payable

        An unused annual exempt amount is wasted and cannot be carried forward to the next tax
        year. Therefore this will have no effect on David's capital gains tax liability.

        The rate of his capital gains tax is 28% once he is a higher rate taxpayer. As a basic rate
        taxpayer to the extent that there is an amount of the basic rate band remaining after
        deducting taxable income, that amount of gains will be taxed at only 18%.

8   A   Partners individually

        The partnership is not taxable in its own right; rather it is an amalgamation of individuals
        effectively taxed as sole traders. Neither are partners taxed jointly. Every individual is liable to
        capital gains tax independently. As the asset is owned by all the partners, each partner must
        declare his share of any gain on his own self-assessment return.

9   Chargeable gain   £   457,840

	£	£
Gross sale proceeds		642,000
Less: original cost (Dec 1997)	176,000	
stamp duty land tax (1% × 176,000)	1,760	
new bathroom	6,400	
		(184,160)
Chargeable gain		457,840

10 A   £10,808

        The painting is a non-wasting chattel and is liable to capital gains tax subject to the chattel
        rules. As it was purchased for less than £6,000 and sold for more than £6,000, there is a
        marginal gain. The gain is the lower of the actual gain and 5/3 × (Gross proceeds - £6,000):

        Actual gain = £14,150 – £142 – £3,200 = £10,808

        5/3 × (£14,150 – £6,000) = £13,583

11 C   A rare collection of snakes worth £320,000

    D   £10,000 of National Savings Certificates

        Shares held in an unquoted trading company are not exempt from capital gains. A diamond
        necklace is a non-wasting asset and is therefore subject to the chattel rules. It is only fully
        exempt if it is both bought and sold for less than £6,000. That clearly would not apply in this
        case. Snakes are a wasting asset and are therefore exempt. National Savings Certificates are
        specifically exempted.

12 C   Gift to a friend of a painting worth £1,000,000

        Gifts on death are not chargeable disposals.

        National Savings Certificates are an exempt asset. As it is not a chargeable asset, there cannot
        be a chargeable disposal.

        A gift of any capital asset to a charity is not a chargeable disposal.

13 B 1 April 2015

The date of disposal for capital gains purposes is the date on which the contract for disposal becomes unconditional. In this case the contract became unconditional on the date the valuation took place. The date contracts are exchanged, legal title passes, physical possession is obtained, or payment is made are all irrelevant.

14 C Assets which are inherited are treated as being acquired by the donee at their value at the time of the donor's death – true

CGT is chargeable on individuals and partners in a partnership. Companies pay corporation tax on their gains.

Stamp duty land tax is an allowable cost on the subsequent disposal of an asset.

Indexation allowance is not available to individuals.

15 B Gain of £2,500 on the disposal of a car – exempt

D Gain of £3,000 on the sale of a greyhound – exempt

A car is an exempt asset.

The greyhound is a wasting chattel and is therefore exempt.

16 A NSPCC, a registered charity. Charities are specifically exempt from CGT.

17 D The gift of an antique table valued at £40,000 to Gordon's daughter on his death

18 C £105,300

Not the repairs as they are not an enhancement expenditure.

£(100,000 + 2,500 + 2,800) = £105,300

19 A Office furniture, purchased for use only in Jack's business office on which he claims capital allowances

C Goodwill of a computer manufacturing business with an expected life of 20 years

An asset used only for business purposes and eligible for capital allowances is specifically treated as a non wasting chattel.

Goodwill is not a chattel as it is not *tangible* moveable property.

20 Javier sold a painting at auction and received £5,900 after deducting auctioneer's fees of £310. The painting had originally cost him £3,500.

A Chargeable – This is a disposal of a non wasting chattel with GROSS sale proceeds of more than £6,000, so chargeable.

Savion received £2,600 for some shares that he sold after deducting £150 of fees. The shares originally cost him £800.

C Chargeable – Shares are not chattels and so not subject to the £6,000 rules.

21 B £500

The brooch is a non-wasting asset and is liable to capital gains tax subject to the chattel rules.

Gain is £(6,200 – 4,000) = £2,200 but restricted to

(Gross sale proceeds – £6,000) × 5/3= (£6,300 – £6,000) × 5/3 = £500

22 D £(900)

	£
Deemed gross sale proceeds	6,000
Less: selling expenses	(200)
Less: cost	(6,700)
Allowable loss	(900)

23   C   A gift of antique jewellery worth £25,000 by Robert, to his daughter as a wedding gift

Disposal to an art gallery is an exempt disposal.

A registered charity is an exempt person.

Gilt-edged securities are an exempt asset.

24   C   Townsend lost an antique ring valued at £8,000, and received a cheque from the insurance company for that sum.

D   Toshi sold a painting for £5,000. It was given to him several years when his grandfather died. At that time it was worth £6,400.

25   Fraser's chargeable gain on disposal of the brooch is £ [1,400]

	£
Gross sale proceeds	8,200
Less auctioneer's fees	(300)
Net sale proceeds	7,900
Less: original cost (July 2000)	(6,100)
enhancement expenditure (September 2004)	(400)
Chargeable gain	1,400

The cost of cleaning and repairs is not capital expenditure. As the brooch was both bought and sold for more than £6,000, the chattel rules do not apply.

26   A   Erwin sold a painting at auction and received £6,100 after deducting auctioneers fees of £200. The painting had originally cost him £3,500.

Chargeable

This is a disposal of a non wasting chattel with gross sale proceeds of more than £6,000, so chargeable.

C   Eryk received £5,900 for jewellery that he sold. The jewellery originally cost him £5,900 plus auctioneers fees of £200.

Chargeable

The total cost of acquiring the jewellery was more than £6,000 (£5,900 + £200), so the disposal is chargeable.

27   B   £500

Gain is (£6,300 – £4,000) = £2,300 but restricted to

(Gross sale proceeds – £6,000) × 5/3= (£6,300 – £6,000) × 5/3 = £500

28   A   £0

Both gross sale proceeds and cost are less than £6,000 so exempt

29   A   An antique diamond necklace worth £3,000 (cost £2,500)

E   Shares held in a NISA

This question is from the sample paper issued by the ICAEW.

30   A   Legal fees on purchase

B   Purchase price

D   Cost of building garage

This question is from the sample paper issued by the ICAEW.

31 A   Gain of £3,600 on the sale of goodwill in her ice cream van business – Chargeable gain

    D   Loss of £2,000 on the sale of a diamond necklace which had cost £4,000 – Exempt

    Goodwill is not a chattel, so cannot be exempt under the £6,000 rule.

    The diamond necklace is a chattel. Gross sale proceeds and cost were less than £6,000

    This question is from the sample paper issued by the ICAEW.

32 C   A gain of £4,200 on the sale of his ten year old racehorse – Decrease. The gain arising on the sale of the race horse is exempt.

    D   Auctioneer's fees of £500 on sale – No effect

    This question is from the sample paper issued by the ICAEW.

33 B   £133,151

	£
Sale proceeds	1,250,100
Less estate agents' fees	(120,000)
Net sale proceeds	1,130,100
Less original cost	(642,000)
Chargeable gain	488,100
Less annual exempt amount	(11,000)
Taxable gain	477,100
CGT liability	
(£31,865 – £27,495) £4,370 × 18%	787
(477,100 – £4,370) × 28%	132,364
	133,151

1   D   0.492

As this is a disposal by a company, indexation runs from the date of acquisition to the date of disposal. For enhancement expenditure, such as an extension, indexation runs from the date of expenditure to the date of disposal. Indexation therefore runs from December 2001 to September 2014:

(258.7 – 173.4)/173.4 = 0.492 (round to 3 decimal places)

2   B   £(12,400)

As a non-wasting asset, the chattel rules apply. As it was sold at a loss, actual proceeds are substituted by deemed proceeds of £6,000 to restrict the loss. No indexation is available as it cannot augment a loss.

	£
Deemed proceeds	6,000
Less selling fees	(400)
Net sale proceeds	5,600
Less cost	(18,000)
Loss	(12,400)

3   B   Gain of £24,000 on the disposal of a rare African snake which had not been used in the business – exempt

C   Gain of £1,100 on the sale of an antique chair. The chair originally cost £5,000 – chargeable gain. The chair is a non-wasting asset which is chargeable. As it was not bought and sold for less than £6,000 (sales proceeds must exceed £6,000 for the level of gain), it is chargeable subject to the chattel rules.

The snake is a wasting asset which is an exempt asset unless it was used in the business and was eligible for capital allowances.

4   Unindexed gain £ [1,604,071]

	£
Sale proceeds	2,125,000
Less disposal costs	(24,969)
Net sale proceeds	2,100,031
Less cost + acquisition costs (£432,000 + £3,000 + £12,960)	(447,960)
Less enhancement expenditure	(48,000)
Unindexed gain	1,604,071

5   A   £55,860

For companies indexation from the date of acquisition to the date of disposal. The indexation factor must be rounded to 3 decimal places.

$$\frac{258.9 - 134.1}{134.1} = 0.931 \times £60,000 = £55,860$$

6   D   £168,800

	£
Sale proceeds	425,000
Cost	(150,000)
Indexation (0.708 × £150,000)	(106,200)
Chargeable gain	168,800

No annual exempt amount for companies.

7   D   Goodwill is a chargeable asset for individuals (but not for companies).

8   C   £3,200

Small companies pay corporation tax at 20%. Companies do not have an annual exempt amount.

20% × £16,000 = £3,200

9   B   1 July 2014 – 31 December 2014

Lettuce Ltd's first accounting period commences when it first acquires a source of income or begins to trade which ever is earlier. In this case opening a building society account means it has acquired a source of income. This first accounting period will, in this case, end when it commences to trade.

Its second accounting period will run from the next day to, in this case, the end of its period of account, ie 1 January 2015 to 30 September 2015. Its third accounting period onwards will be the same as its periods of account.

10   B   Machinery disposal – deduct £1,090

      F   Directors – do not adjust

The profit on disposal is capital related and therefore not treated as part of trading income. As it would originally have been an income item in arriving at the draft trade profits figure, it needs to be deducted to eliminate it.

Directors' emoluments are a valid trading expense even where the directors are also the shareholders. There is no concept of drawings for a company. No adjustment is therefore required.

11   A   Balancing charge – increase trade profits

      E   Donation – reduce trade profits

A balancing charge may arise on the main pool where disposal proceeds of an asset sold exceed the tax written down value brought forward on the pool. Excess capital allowances previously given are reclaimed by adding the balancing charge to trade profits. Trade profits therefore need to be increased by £500.

Charitable donations are normally disallowed in calculating taxable profits. However, where the donation is to a small local charity, it is an allowable trading expense. Trade profits therefore need to be reduced by £100.

12   B   Legal costs – do not adjust

      C   Irrecoverable VAT – adjust

Legal costs relating to the renewal of a short lease (<50 years) is a specifically allowable expense. No adjustment is therefore required.

Irrecoverable VAT is allowable if the item of expenditure to which it relates is also allowable. In this case the car should have been included in the capital allowances computation at its gross value and therefore relief for the irrecoverable VAT will be given over the life of the car. The £3,500 should therefore be added back in calculating the final trade profits figure.

13   B   £12,000

Only the amount actually paid to a registered pension scheme during the accounting period is allowable against trade profits. The £12,000 accrual therefore needs to be added back in order to calculate the final trade profits figure.

14   C   £20,000

Interest is calculated on an accruals basis. Only interest relating to trade is allowable in computing trade profits. Interest on a loan to acquire shares in a subsidiary is not trade related and should be included in loan relationships. Only the interest on the loan to build a factory, including the accrual, is allowed for trade profits.

15　C　£16,456

The stock write-down is specific and is allowable against trade profits. The interest on overdue corporation tax is loss from a non trading loan relationship, not an allowable trading expense.

16　D　£5,600

The trade samples are a business expense and are therefore allowable. As the calendars cost less than £50 each, are not food, alcohol or tobacco, and bear the company logo, they are also allowable.

17　B　£2,592

The maximum capital allowance for a car with CO_2 emissions of between 96g/km and 130g/km for a 12 month accounting period is 18%. The WDA here is £14,400 × 18% = £2,592.

18　Capital allowances £ ⟨ 1,782 ⟩

The balance of the main pool after the disposal of the car is £13,400 – £3,500 = £9,900. The WDA is £9,900 × 18% = £1,782.

19　A　A company with taxable total profits of £1.5m in both the current year and the prior year will pay corporation tax at the main rate.

　　D　The correct marginal relief formula is: fraction × (relevant upper limit – augmented profits) × taxable total profits/augmented profits.

　　　A company with a short accounting period (CAP) must have profits of at least £300,000 *prorated for the number of months in its CAP* before it will pay corporation tax at more than the small profits rate.

　　　A company with five associates will have *the same* limits for the purposes of corporation tax rates compared to the limits for a group of six companies. A company plus its five associates is a group of six so both groups will have the same limits as the limits will be divided by six in both cases.

20　B　£1,018

The correct amount of marginal relief is:

1/400 × (£1,500,000 – £1,050,000) × £950,000/£1,050,000 = £1,018

Deducting taxable total profits instead of augmented profits from the upper limit but then multiplying by taxable total profits/augmented profits gives £1,244. This is incorrect.

Deducting taxable total profits instead of augmented profits from the upper limit and then neglecting to multiply by taxable total profits /augmented profits gives £1,375. This is incorrect.

21　D　£7,000

The amount of corporation tax is Taxable total profits × CT rate. As profits of £35,000 + £8,000 (£7,200 × 100/90) are less than £300,000, the company is small.

1 February 2014 to 31 March 2014 fall in Financial Year 2013 where the corporation tax rate is 20%. 1 April 2014 to 31 January 2015 fall in Financial Year 2014 where the rate is also 20%.

	£
Corporation tax payable	
(£35,000 × 20%)	7,000

22　B　£900

The gross amount charged on the accruals basis is allowable under the loan relationship rules. As the accounting period is 6 months in length, the gross accrued interest is £900 (£20,000 × 9% × 6/12). Remember that it is the gross amount of debenture interest which is included not the net.

23 C £178,500

As this is a six month accounting period the limits need to be prorated. The revised limits are £750,000 and £150,000. Monkey plc therefore needs to pay corporation tax at the main rate of 21%, ie £850,000 × 21% = £178,500.

24 D £8,500

First year allowances at 100% are available to any size of business which purchases a low emission car. First year allowances are never prorated where the accounting period is not 12 months, or where there is private use by an employee.

25 B £5,000

Franked investment income (FII) is gross exempt dividends received from non-associated UK companies. As Giraffe Ltd has a 100% holding in its UK subsidiary the two are associated so the dividends can be ignored. The dividends received from Lion Ltd, however are relevant giving gross FII of £4,500 × 100/90 = £5,000.

26 A A company which is centrally managed and controlled in the UK will always be liable to UK corporation tax on its worldwide profits *is true*.

A company which is incorporated in the UK will only be liable to UK corporation tax on its worldwide profits if it is also centrally managed and controlled in the UK. *This is not true.* If a company is incorporated in the UK it will be liable to UK corporation tax on its worldwide profits regardless of where it is centrally managed and controlled.

A company which is incorporated abroad and centrally managed and controlled abroad will *never* be liable to UK corporation tax on its worldwide profits.

A company which is incorporated abroad will never be liable to UK corporation tax on its worldwide profits *as long as it is also centrally managed and controlled abroad*.

27 C

Non-trading Loan relationships	Trading deduction
£83,000	£42,000

Non-trading loan relationship = £103,000 – £14,000 – £6,000 = £83,000

Trading expenses = £42,000

For companies the interest on the loans to acquire an investment property and a subsidiary company are non-trade related and are therefore included as non-trading loan relationships. Unless a company's trade is financial, all interest receivable is also included in non-trading loan relationships. Allowable interest for trade profits only includes the loan used to purchase a factory.

28 B Neither of them

Budgie Ltd has one associated company. The limits for the purposes of determining the rate of corporation tax are:

Marginal relief upper limit £1,500,000/2 = £750,000

Small profits rate lower limit £300,000/2 = £150,000

Budgie Ltd's taxable total profits of £118,000 and its augmented profits of £145,000 (£118,000 + £27,000) fall below the small profits rate lower limit. Accordingly, Budgie Ltd will pay tax at the small profits rate.

Factor (i) does not affect the company's corporation tax liability. The payment of a dividend is not allowable for the purposes of corporation tax.

Factor (ii) does not affect the company's corporation tax liability. The FII does not change the rate of tax on the taxable total profits as Budgie Ltd pays tax at the small profits rate regardless.

29 C £5,000

£4,600 for the employment contracts is an allowable trading expense. The other two items relate to capital expenditure and are therefore disallowed. Legal costs associated with the acquisition of a short lease (<50 years) are disallowed, although they are allowed for the renewal of a short lease.

30 Maximum capital allowance for the car £ | 2,016 |

Maximum WDA is £16,800 × 18% × 8/12 = £2,016

Note that private use of an asset does not affect capital allowances for a company.

31 C £9,100

AIA covers new machine	£7,000
WDA £20,000 @ 18% × $^7/_{12}$ =	£2,100
	£9,100

32 D £69,500

	£
Trading income	50,000
Chargeable gain	7,500
	57,500
Less qualifying donations	(8,000)
Taxable total profits	49,500
FII £18,000 × 100/90	20,000
Augmented profits	69,500

33 B £149

As Dalmatian Ltd's augmented profits of £1,440,000 (£1,434,060 + £5,940) exceed the small profits rate lower limit of £300,000, it will pay corporation tax at the main rate less marginal relief. The marginal relief is:

Fraction × (upper limit – augmented profits) × taxable total profits/augmented profits

1/400 × (£1,500,000 – £1,440,000) × £1,434,060/£1,440,000 = £149

If you chose C then you subtracted taxable total profits from the upper limit rather than augmented profits.

If you chose D then you ignored franked investment income completely and only used taxable total profits.

34 D 1 August 2014 – 31 January 2015

Airedale Ltd's first accounting period commences when it first acquires a source of income or begins to trade which ever is earlier. In this case opening a building society account means it has acquired a source of income. This first accounting period will, in this case, end when it commences to trade. Its first accounting period is 1 August 2014 – 31 January 2015.

Its second accounting period will run from the next day to, in this case, the end of its period of account ie 1 February 2015 to 30 September 2015.

Its third accounting period onwards will be the same as its periods of account.

35 A Exempt gross dividends received from non-associated UK companies are used to determine a company's corporation tax rate.

D Interest paid on a loan to purchase a new factory is a trading expense.

Companies may *only* deduct qualifying donations *paid* when calculating taxable total profits.

Dividends paid by a company *are an appropriation of profit not a* valid business expense.

Small charitable donations made to *local* charities are allowable against trading income.

36 B £26,000

Franked investment income is gross exempt dividends received from non-associated UK companies, ie Pointer Ltd only. As a wholly owned subsidiary, Doberman Ltd is associated. As Greyhound Ltd was controlled by Dachshund plc at some point in the accounting period it is also an associate.

37 A Depreciation – adjust

C Interest – adjust

As depreciation is a capital item it must be added back to arrive at trading income. Capital allowances will be deducted instead of depreciation.

The interest is not for trading purposes and should be deducted from trading income and included as a non-trading loan relationship credit.

38 A Machinery disposal – add back £4,000

F Redundancy – do not adjust

The loss on disposal is capital related and therefore not allowed as a trading expense. As it would originally have been an expense item in arriving at the draft trading income figure, it needs to be added back to eliminate it.

Redundancy costs are a valid trading expense. No adjustment is therefore required.

39 A Balancing charge – increase trading income by £2,500

F Donation – do not include

A balancing charge may arise on the main pool where disposal proceeds of an asset sold exceed the tax written down value brought forward on the pool. Excess allowances given are reclaimed by adding the balancing charge to trading income. Trading income therefore needs to be increased by £2,500.

Charitable donations are normally included in taxable total profits as a qualifying donation. Only where the donation is to a small local charity, is it an allowable trading expense. In this case it is a donation to an international charity, so it should be excluded from trading income.

40 A £17,000

Only the amount actually paid to a registered pension scheme during the accounting period is allowable against trading income. In the previous year the closing accrual of £17,000 would have been disallowed as it had yet to be paid. As it was paid in the current year it is allowed in the current year. As there is no closing accrual, the full amount of £47,300 has been paid in the current year. Thus the additional £17,000 paid this year which relates to last year needs to be deducted in arriving at trading income.

41 B £13,000

Interest is calculated on an accruals basis. Only interest relating to the trade is allowable in computing trading income. Interest on a loan to acquire an investment is not trade related and should be included in non-trading loan relationships. Only the interest on the loan to purchase new machinery is allowed for trading income.

42 Papillon Ltd's corporation tax liability £ [73,500]

Papillon Ltd has a three month accounting period meaning that the corporation tax limits need to be adjusted. The upper limit is £1.5m × 3/12 = £375,000. As Papillon has taxable total profits + FII of £380,000 it must pay corporation tax at the main rate. Papillon's corporation tax liability is:

£350,000 × 21% = £73,500.

Ensure you multiply taxable total profits, not augmented profits, by 21%.

43 B   £25,667 as a non-trading loan relationship

Debenture interest receivable is assessed on the accruals basis. As the debentures were only owned for two months of the year, the amount assessable is £25,667 ($£1,540,000 \times 10\% \times 2/12$). The fact that no interest was actually received during the accounting period is not relevant. As the debentures are non-trade related (for investment), the interest will be assessed to tax as a non-trading loan relationship credit.

44 C   £43,187

As this is a short accounting period, the limits need to be prorated. The adjusted limits are £1,000,000 and £200,000. Thus Schnauzer plc will pay tax at the main rate less marginal relief:

	£
£215,000 × 21%	45,150
Less: MR $^1/_{400} \times$ (£1,000,000 – £215,000)	(1,963)
Corporation tax payable	43,187

45 A   £1,424

As this is a short accounting period, the limits need to be prorated. The adjusted limits are £1,250,000 and £250,000.

$MR = {}^1/_{400} \times$ (£1,250,000 – £669,000) × 656,000/669,000 = £1,424

Option B uses an unadjusted upper limit of £1.5m.

Option C deducts taxable total profits from the adjusted upper limit but does then multiply by taxable total profits/Augmented profits.

46 D   A company might pay corporation tax at a higher rate if it receives exempt dividends from UK companies in which it has shareholdings of less than 50%.

A company with taxable total profits of less than £1.5 million *may* pay corporation tax at the main rate *if it has franked investment income, a short accounting period or associated companies*.

A company with augmented profits of £300,000 will only pay corporation tax at the small profits rate on its taxable total profits *if it has a 12 month accounting period and no associates*.

A company with no associated companies and a six month accounting period will pay corporation tax at the main rate only if its augmented profits exceed *£750,000*. The six month accounting period means that the upper limit is prorated.

47 B   £7,200

Dividend payments are not a deductible expense for corporation tax purposes. Therefore Whippet plc's corporation tax liability is simply:

£36,000 × 20% = £7,200

48 A   £2,160

The maximum capital allowance for the car for an eight month accounting period is:

£18,000 × 18% × 8/12 = £2,160

49 Capital allowances £ [10,890]

The van is covered by the AIA. The main pool does not exceed £1,000, so may be written off.

Total capital allowances = £10,000 + £890 = £10,890

50   B   Companies with taxable total profits of £1.5m pay corporation tax at the main rate.

The correct marginal relief fraction is:

fraction × (*relevant upper limit* – augmented profits) × taxable total profits /augmented profits.

A group of five companies will have *the same* limits for the purposes of corporation tax rates compared to the limits for a company with four associates. *A company plus its four associates is a group of five so both groups will have the same limits as the limits will be divided by five in both cases.*

A company with a short accounting period (AP) must have augmented profits of at least £300,000 *prorated for the number of months in its AP* before it will pay corporation tax at more than the small profits rate.

51   D   Four

Fouette plc is associated with all the active companies resident anywhere in the world which are under its control. As it has a 50.2% holding in Tutu Ltd, Tutu Ltd is under Fouette plc's control and is associated. Tutu Ltd can control Plie Ltd. As Fouette plc can control Tutu Ltd, it can in turn control Plie Ltd which is therefore also an associate. Pointe SA is also under Fouette plc's control so is also associated regardless of the fact it is resident in France. Brise plc is ignored as it is a dormant company. Thus Fouette plc controls and is associated with Tutu Ltd, Plie Ltd and Pointe SA. There are therefore four associated companies.

52   B   Cloud Ltd and Wind Ltd

In the year ended 31 October 2014 Rain plc does not have control of any of the other companies. A 49% holding in Cloud Ltd means there is no control, which also means Rain plc has no control over Wind Ltd even though Cloud Ltd has an 85% holding. As the holding in Thunder Ltd is not acquired until after the year end, it is also not an associate of Rain plc or any other company for the year in question. Thus the only associated companies are Cloud Ltd and Wind Ltd.

53   D   Assuming all the companies are still actively trading, there are three associates.

Whether a company is owned throughout an accounting period or for only part of an accounting period it will be treated as an associate for the complete accounting period. Subsidiaries should be disposed of at the end of an accounting period rather than at the beginning of the next accounting period to minimise the impact of this rule.

To be considered as an associate a company may be located anywhere in the world, it does not necessarily therefore have to be liable to UK corporation tax.

H's indirect holding in S2 Ltd of 49% *is irrelevant* when considering whether H Ltd and S2 Ltd are associated. The direct holding in S Ltd is 75% which means H Ltd controls S Ltd. As S Ltd in turn controls S2 Ltd, H Ltd controls both S Ltd and S2 Ltd. H Ltd can direct S Ltd as to how to use its controlling votes in S2 Ltd, therefore H Ltd controls S2 Ltd.

54   D   £187,500 and £37,500

As Mountain Ltd's parent company has two other wholly owned subsidiaries, there are four associated companies: Parent + Mountain Ltd + two other subsidiaries. The revised limits become £375,000 and £75,000.

As Mountain Ltd has also prepared its accounts for a six month period, the limits need to be further prorated to account for the short accounting period:

£375,000 × 6/12 = £187,500

£75,000 × 6/12 = £37,500.

55 B £1,071

	Y/e 31 March 2015 £
Taxable total profits	1,000,000
FII	50,000
Augmented profits	1,050,000
	Marginal relief applies

Marginal relief

(£1,500,000 – £1,050,000) × £1,000,000/£1,050,000 × 1/400   <u>1,071</u>

56 C £862,050

Precipice plc has taxable total profits of £4,105,000 ie £4,000,000 + £25,000 + £95,000 – £15,000. Therefore it pays corporation tax at 21%. Only the qualifying donation actually paid in the year is deducted as a qualifying charitable donation.

57 B £305,125

	Y/e 30 November 2014 £
Taxable total profits	1,410,000
FII	0
Augmented profits	1,410,000
	Marginal relief applies
FY13 4/12 × £1,410,000 × 23%	108,100
FY14 8/12 × £1,410,000 × 21%	197,400
Less marginal relief	
FY13 4/12 × (£1,500,000 – £1,410,000) × 3/400	(225)
FY14 8/12 × (£1,500,000 – £1,410,000) × 1/400	(150)
Corporation tax payable	305,125

The year ended 30 November 2014 straddles two financial years (FY13 and FY14). As the rates of tax changed on 1 April 2014 the taxable total profits need to be split between the two financial years. When calculating marginal relief, because the fraction has changed between FY13 and FY14 the calculation must be done in two parts.

Alternatively the marginal relief could be calculated as follows:

	FY2013 £	FY2014 £
	4/12	8/12
Taxable total profits/Augmented profits	470,000	940,000
Upper limit	500,000	1,000,000
Lower limit	100,000	200,000
Marginal relief		
FY2013 (£500,000 – £470,000) × 3/400	(225)	
FY2014 (£1,000,000 – £940,000) × 1/400		(150)

58 B £22,500

The gross amount charged on the accruals basis is allowable as a loan relationship debit. As the accounting period is 9 months in length, the gross accrued interest is £22,500 (£600,000 × 5% × 9/12). Remember that it is the gross amount of debenture interest which is included, not the net.

59 D A company which is incorporated in the UK but not centrally managed and controlled in the UK, will still be liable to UK corporation tax on its worldwide profits.

A company which is not incorporated in the UK nor centrally managed and controlled in the UK, will *not* be liable to UK corporation tax on its worldwide profits.

A company which is not incorporated in the UK will never be liable to UK corporation tax on its worldwide profits *as long as it is not centrally managed and controlled from the UK.*

A company which is not centrally managed and controlled in the UK will never be liable to UK corporation tax on its worldwide profits *as long as it is also not incorporated in the UK.*

60 C £4,600

The costs associated with renting out the top floor are not business related and are therefore not allowed for trading income purposes. As two floors of the office building are used in the company's trade, two thirds of the loan interest is allowed as a trading expense.
The remaining interest is a loss on loan relationships as it is not trade related. The allowable expense is £3,000 × 2/3 + £3,900 × 2/3 = £4,600.

61 B Loss on sale of two cars – exempt

D Gain on sale of an investment property – chargeable gain

This question is from the sample paper issued by the ICAEW.

62 Unindexed gain £ | 119,900 |

	£
Proceeds	312,000
Less: Cost	(165,000)
Fees (£2,450 + £1,650)	(4,100)
Extension	(23,000)
Unindexed gain	119,900

The repair is not enhancement expenditure.

This question is from the sample paper issued by the ICAEW.

63 A Depreciation of the office building – add back

F Entertaining staff at a party which costs £85 per head – no adjustment

This question is from the sample paper issued by the ICAEW.

64 A Employer's national insurance contributions

E Replacement of roof tiles

Gifts of food, drink or tobacco are disallowed. Interest on a loan to purchase shares in a subsidiary and interest on overdue corporation tax are expenses in arriving at profits on non-trading loan relationships.

This question is from the sample paper issued by the ICAEW.

65 Capital allowances on the low emission car £ | 13,500 |

FYA @ 100% × £13,500 = £13,500

This question is from the sample paper issued by the ICAEW.

66 Capital allowances on the computer £ | 6,900 |

AIA is available to cover the purchase of the computer.

This question is from the sample paper issued by the ICAEW.

67   Capital allowances on the main pool £ `33,000`

	£
TWDV b/f	54,000
Additions (AIA)	6,900
AIA	(6,900)
Additions – car	16,000
	70,000
WDA @ 18%	(12,600)
TWDV c/f	57,400

There is no private use restriction in respect of a *company's* capital allowances.

The total allowances due are AIA of £6,900 + FYA of £13,500 + WDA of £12,600 = £33,000

This question is from the sample paper issued by the ICAEW.

68   D   Interest payable on a loan to purchase an investment property

       E   Interest payable on a loan to purchase shares in Dim Ltd, another trading company

This question is from the sample paper issued by the ICAEW.

69   B   A qualifying donation to charity – Decrease

       D   Recovery of previously written off trade debts – Increase

This question is from the sample paper issued by the ICAEW.

70   B   £306,788 (£225,677 + (100/90 × £73,000))

This question is from the sample paper issued by the ICAEW.

71   Corporation tax payable £ `228,515`

The marginal rate upper limit for the nine month period is £1,500,000 × 9/12 = £1,125,000

	£
£1,088,600 × 21%	228,606
Less: Marginal relief (£1,125,000 – £1,088,600) × $\dfrac{1}{400}$	(91)
	228,515

This question is from the sample paper issued by the ICAEW.

72   B   1 February 2013 to 31 January 2014

       A corporation tax accounting period cannot exceed 12 months in length.

       This question is from the sample paper issued by the ICAEW.

73   Corporation tax payable £ `52,000`

	Y/e 31 December 2014
	£
Taxable total profits	260,000
FII	20,000
Augmented profits	280,000

Small profits rate applies

FY13 and FY14 small profits rate is 20%
Corporation tax payable:
£260,000 × 20%   52,000

74 D £298,660

	P/e 30 September 2014 £
Taxable total profits	1,370,000
FII	-
Augmented profits	1,370,000

Marginal relief upper limit (£1,500,000 × 10/12) = £1,250,000

Small profits rate lower limit (£300,000 × 10/12) = £250,000

Main rate applies

FY13 4/10 × £1,370,000 × 23%	126,040
FY14 6/10 × £1,370,000 × 21%	172,620
Corporation tax payable	298,660

1 B 8 May

The time the goods are made available – invoice not issued within 14 days

2 D Entertaining costs of UK business customers

Van accessories – business assets – OK

Partitioning and motor cycle – business assets – OK

Entertaining – statutory disallowance of input tax except for entertaining employees and foreign customers

3 A Demonstrate that he intends to make either zero or standard rated supplies or both.

A person not required to be registered must be registered if he so requests and if HMRC is satisfied that he makes taxable supplies (standard and/or zero rated) or is carrying on a business and intends to make taxable supplies.

4 C He must register, based on turnover of standard and zero rated supplies, which exceed £81,000.

Registration limit is in relation to taxable supplies, defined as standard and zero rated supplies (and reduced rate supplies if any).

5 A £180.00

£1,000 less 10% discount   £900.00 (assume maximum discount applies)

VAT thereon @ 20%   £180.00

6 B 30 March 2015

First twelve-month period in which £81,000 limit exceeded is y/e 28 February 2015. Total = £82,100

Notification is required thirty days after the end of month in which limit is exceeded, ie 30 March 2015.

7 B £65.17

Fuel scale rate = £391 × $\dfrac{1}{6}$ = £65.17 per quarter

8 C £64

	£
Hotel accommodation costs reimbursed deductible	64
Flat rate subsistence is remuneration, so outside scope	–
Input tax recoverable	64

9 B £5,425

VAT may be reclaimed on vehicles (new or second-hand) other than cars used privately.

	£
On van (£9,450 × $\dfrac{1}{6}$)	1,575
On lorry (£23,100 × $\dfrac{1}{6}$)	3,850
	5,425

10 A The debtor does not need to be formally insolvent.

11   A   1 February

The basic tax point is the date that the goods are despatched to Tariq, ie 8 February.

However, where the supplier issues an invoice or receives payment before the basic tax point, the earlier date becomes the actual tax point. So in this case as both the invoice and the payment occur before the basic tax point, the earlier of these two dates becomes the actual tax point, ie 1 February when the invoice is issued.

12   B   £400.00

A gift of business assets is a deemed supply for VAT purposes, unless it is a trade sample or the cost of gifts made to the same person in a 12 month period does not exceed £50.

The gift of the laptop is therefore a deemed supply. The value of the supply is the VAT exclusive cost Quentin would have had to pay at the time of the supply to replace the laptop, ie £2,000.

The output VAT to be accounted for by Quentin is £2,000 × 20% = 400.00

13   B   Two

A 'person' for VAT purposes includes an individual sole trader, partnership, limited company, club, association or charity. A person's registration covers all of his business activities, however diverse. It is the 'person' who is registered, not the business.

Therefore, Valerie will register as a sole trader (with two businesses) and the partnership will have a separate registration.

14   C   £302.40

VAT is calculated after both trade discount and cash discounts, irrespective of whether payment is made within the specified time period. Therefore VAT on invoice is £302.40 (£1,512 @ 20%).

15   A   4 May

As the payment is received before the basic tax point date (BTPD) ie despatch, the date of payment becomes the actual tax point date. It is worth noting here that the invoice was issued within 14 days of the BTPD and this would then normally have become the tax point unless payment is made before the invoice date.

16   B   29 June 2015 to notify HMRC

      D   31 May 2015 to start charging VAT

Priscilla must notify HMRC by the end of the 30-day period for which it is believed the threshold will be exceeded. Under the future prospects test registration takes effect from the beginning of the 30-day period.

17   C   Use of car for her wedding only

The gift of services (to the cousin or anyone else) is specifically not a taxable supply. As opposed to a gift of goods which is a deemed supply.

The private use of goods owned by a business and the private use of services, supplied to the business, by the owner are taxable supplies.

18   C   2 April

As an invoice is issued within fourteen days of the basic tax point ie despatch, the date on which the invoice is issued becomes the actual tax point. The end of the quarter does not affect this.

19 C £10,310

	£
Invoice total including VAT	10,470
Less road fund licence	(160)
	10,310

VAT on motor cars with any amount of private use is irrecoverable; it is therefore included in the capital cost for capital allowance purposes.

20 B A tax invoice is held

To be recoverable the goods or services must be used for business purposes and the input VAT must be supported by a VAT invoice.

21 C £80

VAT in respect of lunches on business trips is recoverable ($£480 \times \dfrac{1}{6} = £80$)

22 A Both businesses

A 'person' for VAT purposes includes an individual sole trader, partnership, limited company, club, association or charity. A person's registration covers all of his business activities, however diverse. It is the 'person' who is registered, not the business.

Therefore, Parminder will register as a sole trader with two businesses and will have to charge VAT to the customers of both businesses.

23 B 2 March to notify HMRC

D 1 February to start charging VAT

Sheep plc must notify HMRC by the end of the 30 day period for which it is believed the threshold will be exceeded, ie by 2 March. Under the future prospects test registration takes effect from the beginning of the thirty-day period.

24 C Deregistration will be effective immediately and must be notified by 30 March 2015

Cow plc must deregister as it is no longer making taxable supplies. A wholly exempt trader cannot be registered for VAT. The registration will be effective immediately but Cow plc has 30 days in which to notify HMRC, ie by 30 March.

25 B £165.67

VAT collected = $(£400 \times 20\%) + (£514 \times \dfrac{1}{6}) = £165.67$.

26 What is the correct amount of output VAT to be charged? £ ⬚ 192 ⬚

$£1,000 \times 96\% \times 20\% = £192$.

VAT is calculated on the price of the supply less the maximum discount even if the discount is not taken up.

27 What is the amount of output VAT to be charged? £ ⬚ 91 ⬚

As Courgette Ltd claims back all the input VAT relating to its fuel, all the input tax paid is recoverable. However it must also use the fuel scale charges to calculate the amount of output tax it must account for to offset the private use element of the fuel:

Output VAT charge = Fuel scale charge = $£548 \times \dfrac{1}{6} = £91$ per quarter.

28 A UK client entertaining

E Company car for employee use which is a taxable benefit for income tax purposes

The VAT on UK client entertaining is never recoverable. The VAT on a company car with private use by an employee is also irrecoverable. For the car to qualify as a taxable benefit there must be private use.

The VAT on fuel in company pool cars is recoverable. VAT on capital purchases for business use is always recoverable. As a pre-registration purchase, it must still be owned at registration and have been purchased within four years pre registration. VAT on gifts of goods to customers is recoverable although output VAT must be charged as a deemed supply.

29 C 30 July 2015

Wayne must register for VAT once his taxable turnover for the prior 12 months exceeds the VAT registration threshold. This happens during the month to 30 June 2015 when his turnover reaches £82,600. He is therefore liable to notify his liability by 30 July 2015.

30 A £770

VAT may be recovered on all three items. The VAT on the van may be recovered as it is still held in the business at the time of registration and was purchased within four years of registration. The same applies to the stock of spare parts. The invoice for accountancy services is dated no more than six months before the date of registration and is therefore also recoverable.

31 B VAT is chargeable on zero rated supplies, at 0%.

A trader who is wholly exempt may not register for VAT. VAT at the standard rate is charged at 20%. A trader making taxable supplies may voluntarily register for VAT even where taxable supplies are below the VAT registration threshold.

32 A 30 December 2014

As Michael's turnover is £82,200 for the 12 months ended 30 November 2014, he must notify HMRC within 30 days, ie by 30 December 2014.

33 C Miranda may choose to deregister but would then need to repay input VAT recovered on stock and capital items still held at deregistration if the input VAT exceeds £1,000.

As Miranda's taxable supplies are now below the registration threshold and her forecast taxable turnover is below the deregistration threshold, she may choose to deregister. She may remain registered if she prefers, as she still makes some taxable supplies.

On deregistration, there is a deemed supply of trade stock and capital items on which VAT has previously been recovered. Output VAT is payable on this deemed supply subject to it being greater than £1,000.

34 C Gifts of services worth £100 each to a customer.

Gifts of services are never a deemed supply. Gifts of business assets worth less than £50 per annum per recipient are not a deemed supply.

35 A £256

In order to recover input VAT on purchases the item must be for business purposes and be supported by a valid VAT invoice. Only the VAT on the office stationery is therefore recoverable.

36 B A gift of business services is not a taxable supply.

Where discounts are available, the amount of VAT should be calculated based on all potential discounts available. The VAT should not be adjusted later if all potential discounts are not actually taken up.

The value of the supply of a business asset used for private purposes is the cost to the taxable person of providing the asset.

VAT fuel scale charges are used to calculate the output VAT payable on the deemed supply of private fuel for motoring.

37   D   31 March 2015

In order to recover output VAT on an unpaid invoice, the debt must be more than six months old and the debt must have been written off in the accounts. Six months from the due date of payment of 31 August 2014 is 28 February 2015. However, as the debt is not written off in Flight plc's accounts until 31 March 2015, that becomes the earliest date that Flight plc could make a claim to recover the unpaid output VAT.

38   A   1 September

The basic tax point is the date that the goods are despatched to Sunil, ie 8 September.

However, where the supplier issues an invoice before the basic tax point, ie on 1 September, this date becomes the actual tax point.

39   C   1 November

Basic tax point for goods on sale or return is the adoption date (maximum of 12 months later) – so 1 November. Invoice date is more than 14 days later so actual tax point is the basic tax point.

40   C   29 October

Basic tax point is the date the goods are made available to the customer (18 October). However actual tax point is invoice date (29 October) as it is less than 14 days after the basic tax point.

41   C   Disco Ltd must be making or intending to make some taxable supplies.

The alternative answers are incorrect because:

The company can register if it makes a mixture of taxable and exempt supplies.

It is advantageous to register if expecting to be in a repayment position but it is not required.

The company does not have to be expecting to exceed the VAT threshold.

42   B   The company is required to notify HMRC of its liability to register by 30 November 2014

F   Registration takes effect from 1 December 2014

Under the historic turnover test, a trader must notify HMRC within 30 days of the end of the month in which the threshold was exceeded. Registration is effective from the first of the month after the end of the month following the threshold being exceeded.

43   C   No, based on taxable supplies of normal trading

Include taxable supplies to determine whether the threshold is exceeded, but exclude supplies of capital assets.

44   B   £244

Accommodation	64
Laptop (business use)	180
	244

The meals are part of salary hence outside the scope. The laptop is provided as part of an employee's remuneration package and is a valid expense of the business. Therefore there is no restriction for private use.

45   B   £1,680

VAT is irrecoverable on motor cars where there is private use, hence recoverable on the van only.

$(1/6 \times £10,080) = £1,680$

46 A period of six months has elapsed since the goods were supplied.

    B   Incorrect

        Tax on the supply has been accounted for and paid.

    C   Correct

        The bad debt claim must be made within six years of becoming eligible for relief.

    F   Incorrect

        A period of six months must have elapsed since the *due date for payment*.

        The bad debt claim must be made within **four** years of becoming eligible for relief.

47 B   £1,152

        Maximum discount 10% = £5,760 × 20% = £1,152

48 A   3 April

        If payment is received before the basic tax point, payment date is the actual tax point.

49 Steve, who is registered for VAT, runs a plant hire company. In the quarter ended 31 March 2015 he let his brother use a digger at no charge.

    B   Not taxable

        A gift of services is not a taxable supply

        In the quarter to 30 June 2015 he used the same digger to help dig the foundations for the extension being built onto his house.

    C   Taxable

        Goods owned by a business and temporarily used by the owner are a taxable supply.

50 A   £25,380

        Input tax is not recoverable on cars and accessories fitted when supplied, where the car is not used 100% for business.

51 D   £100.00

        VAT-exclusive price payable by the person supplying the asset to purchase an identical replacement (ie at cost).

52 D   £71.33 reclaimable

	£
Output tax (1/6 × £517)	86.17
Input tax (1/6 × £945)	(157.50)
Reclaimable	(71.33)

53 Wood Ltd still owes £5,000 from an invoice issued on 30 June 2014. Gertrude still believes that the amount will be paid in full and so it has not been written off in the accounts.

    B   Bad debt relief cannot be claimed

    Trees Ltd owes £2,000 from an invoice issued on 15 September 2014. Gertrude does not expect payment of this and has written it off in the accounts.

    D   Bad debt relief cannot be claimed

    Wood Ltd – not written off so not reclaimable

    Trees Ltd – not yet 6 months since *payment* due (15 October 2014)

54 A   Only the goods used in Jacob's house are a taxable supply

ICAEW

55 A business making £45,000 of standard rated supplies and £37,000 of exempt supplies is required to VAT register.

    B   Incorrect – VAT registration is required if *taxable* turnover exceeds £81,000 ie exclude exempt turnover.

A business making £82,000 of zero rated supplies only does not have to become VAT registered.

    C   Correct – A business making purely zero rated supplies can apply for exemption from registration.

56   C   1 March 2015

    From the first day after the end of the month following the cumulative turnover exceeding £81,000.

    It exceeds the limit at the end of January 2015 (5 × £4,900) + (6 × £7,600) + £11,000 = £81,100. So VAT registered from 1 March 2015.

57 It must notify HMRC of its liability to VAT register by

    B   30 January 2015

The company's VAT registration is effective from

    D   1 January 2015

Future prospects rule – 30 days to notify – 30 January 2015

                       – immediate liability to charge VAT – 1 January 2015

58   A   £12.67

    C   Payable by Maddie

    Maddie is liable for the VAT that should have been paid on the sale. The consideration received by Maddie is deemed to be VAT-inclusive.

    Therefore the amount of output VAT payable is £76 × 1/6 = £12.67

59   B   Exempt supplies – Do not include

    D   Supply of surplus office machinery – Do not include

This question is from the sample paper issued by the ICAEW.

60   C   Machine with no VAT invoice – Not recoverable

    F   Purchase of car – Not recoverable

This question is from the sample paper issued by the ICAEW.

61   B   Quarter to 28 February 2015 – £192

    E   Quarter to 31 May 2015 – £1,725

This question is from the sample paper issued by the ICAEW.

62   A   Amount of VAT payable – £16.67

    C   VAT is payable by David

This question is from the sample paper issued by the ICAEW.

63   B   A trader can voluntarily register for VAT if he makes only zero rated supplies.

    C   A trader making both zero rated and standard rated supplies is required to register only if the level of taxable supplies exceeds the VAT registration limit.

This question is from the sample paper issued by the ICAEW.

64 Output VAT £ [5,912]

Output VAT

£29,560 × 20% = £5,912

This question is from the sample paper issued by the ICAEW.

65 Input VAT £ [3,030]

£(900 + 2,130)

This question is from the sample paper issued by the ICAEW.

66 C 30 December 2014

	£
Turnover	
January to August (£6,150 × 8)	49,200
September/October	21,000
November	11,000
	81,200

The VAT registration limit is therefore exceeded at the end of November.

This question is from the sample paper issued by the ICAEW.

1   C   7 May 2015

      F   7 May 2015

        A VAT return is filed electronically and due 7 days after the end of the month following the end of the return period. Payment must also be made electronically and the deadline is the same.

2   D   Two payments of £125,000 each and a balancing payment of £650,000

        A trader with an annual VAT liability in excess of £2.3m is known as a 'substantial trader' and is required to make payments on account (POA) during each quarter. The POA are made in months 2 and 3 of each quarter with a balancing payment made one month after the quarter end. The payments required from Cornflower plc are:

	£
28 February 2015 = 1/24 × £3,000,000	125,000
31 March 2015= 1/24 × £3,000,000	125,000
30 April 2015 = balancing payment due for the quarter ended 31 March 2015	650,000
	900,000

3   C   £250

        If a less detailed VAT invoice is to be issued, the maximum consideration permitted is £250.

4   A   A VAT invoice must be issued to all taxable and non-taxable customers.

      C   A less detailed invoice may be issued if the VAT inclusive sale proceeds are less than £150.

        A VAT invoice must be issued to all taxable customers, but it is not necessary to issue a VAT invoice to non taxable customers, although an invoice often is issued in practice.

        A less detailed invoice may be issued if the VAT inclusive sale proceeds are not more than £250.

5   D   She pays her VAT in nine monthly instalments starting in April 2014 with a balancing payment and the return submitted by 28 February 2015.

6   D   £4,500 by 31 May 2015

        Nine payments on account equal to 1/10 of the previous year's VAT liability are made. Any balancing payment and the VAT return are due two months after the end of the year.

7   D   Both

        Taxable persons must keep records of all transactions to support both the output VAT charged and the claim for recoverable input VAT.

8   B   £1,350,000

        The annual accounting scheme is available if the value of taxable supplies (excluding VAT and supplies of capital items) does not exceed £1,350,000.

9   C   Each payment on account is 1/24 of the total VAT liability of the previous year.

        Under the VAT payment on accounts scheme, large traders (VAT annual liability > £2.3m) make monthly payments on account. Within each quarter, VAT equivalent to 1/24 of the previous year's VAT liability is payable in months 2 and 3. One month after the end of each quarter the balance, if any, for that quarter is payable. Thus for a trader with a December year end payments will be made from January to December. The payment for January will relate to the previous quarter and the other eleven payments will relate to the current year. The 7 day extension does not apply to the payments on account scheme.

10 B Businesses operating the flat rate scheme apply their sector percentage to total (both taxable and exempt) VAT inclusive turnover.

   C HMRC may grant exemption from registration to zero rated traders that have negligible amounts of input VAT.

       Businesses with an annual VAT *liability* in excess of £2.3m must join the VAT payments on account scheme.

       The main advantage of the annual accounting scheme is the need to only file *one annual VAT return*.

       Businesses operating the cash accounting scheme may also join the annual accounting scheme and *vice versa*.

11 C The scheme is advantageous for businesses making only zero rated supplies

   E Businesses in the scheme must leave if taxable supplies in the previous 12 months exceed £1.35m.

       Businesses making zero rated supplies only reclaim input tax – the reclaim will not be sooner using cash accounting.

       A business must leave the cash accounting scheme if taxable supplies in the previous 12 months exceed £1.6m.

12 A trader may join the annual accounting scheme where the taxable turnover in the following year is not expected to exceed £ | 1,350,000 |

13 B £550,000

       Monthly instalments £3m/24 = £125,000

       Balance due one month after quarter end = £(800,000 – 125,000 – 125,000) = £550,000

14 B Automatic bad debt relief is given.

       This is a feature of the cash accounting scheme.

15 A Businesses calculate VAT due as a flat rate percentage of their VAT exclusive turnover.

       The VAT is calculated on the VAT **inclusive** turnover.

16 D £1,122

       The flat rate percentage is applied to the total (both taxable and exempt) turnover of the business inclusive of VAT, ie £8,500 × 1.20 × 11% = £1,122.

17 C £2,008

       As Florence Ltd operates the cash accounting scheme its tax point is the date of payment to suppliers or the date of receipt of payment from customers. Hence any input tax which is paid in the quarter is also recoverable in the quarter. VAT on the artwork and the marketing literature is therefore recoverable in this quarter. VAT on the spare machinery parts will be recovered in the next quarter.

18 D 4 June

       Since Gordon is a member of the cash accounting scheme output VAT is accounted for when the payment is received from the customer.

19 D Within the flat rate scheme, output VAT is calculated as the relevant business % × VAT inclusive turnover. There is no recovery of input VAT. Therefore Tony's VAT payable to HMRC is £17,000 × 1.20 × 8% = £1,632.

20 B A trader using the flat rate scheme may also be authorised to use the annual accounting scheme.

   D Where a customer requires an invoice, a flat rate trader who makes wholly standard rated supplies will issue a VAT invoice showing 20% output tax.

       This question is from the sample paper issued by the ICAEW.

21 B Automatic bad debt relief is given

   C Output VAT is accounted for when cash is received from the customer.

       This question is from the sample paper issued by the ICAEW.

Chapter 13: Administration of tax

1   A   5 October 2014

       A taxpayer is required to notify HMRC of the need to complete a self assessment return by 5 October following the tax year in which a new source of income is acquired. As Camilla commenced to trade in 2013/14 she is required to notify by 5 October 2014.

2   C   15 March 2016

       A taxpayer who wishes to submit a tax return online must do so by the later of 31 January following the tax year end and three months from the date the return was issued.

3   A   Short tax return

       C   Short tax return

       A taxpayer who is an employee but not a director, a sole trader with a turnover of less than £81,000 per annum or a pensioner is not required to submit a full tax return each year. The taxpayer may however, decide to continue to submit a full tax return in any event. This is voluntary and not a requirement unless the taxpayer is sent a full return by HMRC or wants to submit online.

4   B   31 January 2021

       C   31 January 2017

       Because he has a business, Edward must keep records (of whatever nature) for his 2014/15 tax return until 31 Jan 2021. Records where a taxpayer has a business must be kept for five years from the 31 January following the end of the tax year to which they relate.

       Where a taxpayer is not in business (ie the records are purely personal), the records must be kept for one year from the 31 January following the end of the tax year to which they relate, ie 31 January 2017.

5   C   31 January 2016

       A return may be amended for any reason within 12 months of when the return should have been filed, not when it was actually filed. A return relating to 2013/14 should have been filed by 31 January 2015. The amendment must therefore be made by 31 January 2016.

6   B   31 January 2015, 31 July 2015 and 31 January 2016

       A sole trader who is not in his first year is required to make payments on account. Eugenie must therefore make payments on account on 31 January in the tax year and 31 July following the tax year end. A final balancing payment is made on 31 January following the tax year end.

7   Payment on account   £   5,500

Harry's payments on account (POA) for 2014/15 will be half of the income tax and class 4 NICs paid under self assessment in 2013/14:

	£
Income tax liability for 2013/14	15,000
Less income tax deducted at source	(6,000)
	9,000
Plus NIC class 4 for 2013/14	2,000
	11,000
× 50%	5,500

Payments on account are not due in respect of capital gains tax.

8   C   All of the payments were made late and will be liable to interest from the due date to the day before payment but only the balancing payment is liable to a penalty at 5%

Sophie's payments should have been made on 31 January 2015, 31 July 2015 and 31 January 2016. They were all late and will be liable to interest from the due date to the day before payment. In addition the balancing payment is potentially liable to a penalty. Where it is paid more than 30 days late (the penalty date), the penalty is 5%. Where it is paid more than six months after the payment due date, ie after 2 August, there is a further penalty of 5%.

9   C   5 October 2015

A taxpayer is required to notify HMRC of the need to complete a self assessment return by 5 October following the tax year in which a new source of income is acquired. As Albert commenced to trade in 2014/15 he is required to notify by 5 October 2015.

10   D   31 January 2021 – five years after the 31 January following 2014/15 (5 years after 31 January 2016)

11   A   By 30 November 2015 if he wants HMRC to calculate his tax

        E   By 31 January 2016 if he wants to file online

If HMRC is to calculate the tax liability, the normal due date for filing the tax return is 31 October following the end of the tax year.

However, where the notice to make a return is issued after 31 July following the end of the tax year, the deadline is extended to three months after the issue of the notice if the taxpayer calculates their own tax liability, or the deadline is extended by two months after the issue of the notice if HMRC are to calculate the tax, ie 30 November 2015 in this case.

If the taxpayer is to file online, the normal due date for filing the tax return is 31 January following the end of the tax year.

Where the notice to make a return is issued after 31 October following the end of the tax year, the deadline is extended to three months after the issue of the notice – not relevant in this case.

12   A   Elaine can amend her tax return on 15 December 2016

        C   Elaine can make a claim for overpayment relief because there is an error in her return on 31 December 2018

A taxpayer can amend his/her tax return any time before 12 months after 31 January following the tax year, ie before 31 January 2017 for a 2014/15 return issued on 6 May 2015. Elaine can therefore amend her tax return on 15 December 2016.

HMRC can correct any obvious errors or mistakes in a taxpayer's tax return within nine months of the date the return is filed, ie 1 September 2016 for a return filed on 1 December 2015. HMRC cannot therefore correct an arithmetical error in Elaine's return on 29 September 2016.

A taxpayer can make a claim for overpayment relief within four years of the end of the tax year, ie before 5 April 2019 for 2014/15. Elaine can therefore make a claim on 31 December 2018 that there is an error in her return.

HMRC can give notice of an enquiry into a return until 12 months after the actual filing date of the return ie 12 months after 1 December 2015. Therefore notice cannot be given on 20 December 2016.

13   If HMRC wishes to collect the unpaid tax, it must raise an assessment by 5 April   2019

Where the taxpayer has made an incomplete disclosure of facts in his tax return, which is not due to careless or deliberate behaviour, HMRC has until four years after the end of the tax year to raise a discovery assessment, ie 5 April 2019 for 2014/15.

14 A £0

Tax payable for 2013/14

	£
Total tax liability	28,450
Paid under PAYE	(23,400)
Balance payable under self assessment	5,050

The balance payable by self assessment re 2013/14 is 17.75% (£5,050 ÷ £28,450) of the total income tax liability for that year. As this is less than 20% of the total tax liability, payments on account are not required in 2014/15.

Therefore no payment on account of Harriet's 2014/15 tax liability should have been paid on 31 July 2015.

15 On 31 January 2015, to avoid interest charges, Ivan should have paid tax of £ | 9,350 |

The tax due on 31 January 2015 is calculated as follows.

	£	£
Balancing payment for 2013/14		
Total tax liability	15,500	
Class 4 NICs	3,200	
Paid under PAYE/tax credits	(3,800)	
Tax paid by self assessment	14,900	
Payments on account	(13,000)	
		1,900
Payment on account for 2014/15		
50% of tax paid by self assessment for 2013/14 (50% × £14,900)		7,450
Tax due on 31 January 2015		9,350

16 C £6,600

Tax payable for 2013/14

	£	£
Total income tax liability	18,200	
Paid under PAYE/tax credits	(5,000)	
Balance paid by self assessment	13,200	
Payment on account for 2014/15 due 31 July 2015		
50% of tax paid by self assessment for 2013/14 (50% × £13,200)		6,600

Payments on account are not required in respect of capital gains tax. Capital gains tax is settled via one payment on 31 January following the end of the tax year.

17 B £190

A penalty of 5% of the tax overdue is payable where income tax, Class 4 NICs and capital gains tax are paid more than 30 days after the due date. Penalties do not, however, apply to payments on account.

Where the tax is still outstanding six months after the payment due date a further 5% of the tax overdue is charged.

The balancing payment for income tax paid late is £1,500 (£9,500 – £8,000 POA) and the capital gains tax of £2,300 is also paid late.

Kurt will therefore be liable for a penalty of £190, being 5% of the total amount paid late of £3,800 (£1,500 + £2,300), which was due on 31 January 2015.

18 Interest will run on the additional liability of £1,500 from 1 April 2015 to 14 May 2015

    B   False

    A penalty of £75 is payable by Martha

    C   True

    Interest on discovery assessments runs from the due filing date (31 January 2015 for 2013/14) until the day before the tax is paid. The first statement is therefore not true.

    A penalty of £75, being 5% of £1,500, will apply to the additional tax arising from a discovery assessment. The second statement is therefore true.

19 An appeal against a discovery assessment must be made in writing within a calendar month of the date of the assessment

    B   False – An appeal against a discovery assessment must be made in writing within 30 days of the date of the assessment. Therefore the statement is not true.

    The taxpayer must first apply for an internal review before making an appeal to the First-tier Tribunal.

    D   False – An internal review is optional.

    A taxpayer can appeal against and apply to postpone the tax due under an assessment raised as a result of an enquiry into a tax return.

    E   True

20 B   5 October 2015

    Where HMRC does not issue a tax return it must be notified of chargeable gains arising by 5 October following the end of the tax year in which the gain arose.

21 C   5 April 2035

    HMRC may raise a discovery assessment where full disclosure has not been made either due to negligence or fraud at any time up until 20 years after the end of the tax year.

22 A   £6,570

    The tax paid by self assessment in 2013/14 is

	£
Total tax liability	15,320
Bank interest tax deducted	(2,000)
Dividend tax credit ($£1,620 \times \frac{100}{90} \times 10\%$)	(180)
Tax payable under self assessment	13,140

    The payment on account due on 31 January 2015 is 50% of the previous year's tax paid by self assessment, ie £13,140 × 50% = £6,570.

23 A   £0

    Tax payable for 2013/14

	£
Total income tax liability	23,200
Paid under PAYE/tax credits	(19,000)
Balance payable under self assessment	4,200

    The balance payable by self assessment re 2013/14 is 18.1% (£4,200 ÷ £23,200) of the total income tax liability for that year. As this is less than 20% of the total tax liability, payments on account are not required in 2014/15.

    Payments on account are not required in respect of capital gains tax. Capital gains tax is settled via one payment on the 31 January following the end of the tax year.

    Therefore no payment on account of Greg's 2014/15 liability should have been paid on 31 July 2015.

24 Harold is due to make a payment on 31 July 2015. To minimise any interest charges you would advise that he makes a payment on that date of £ [9,700]

Tax payable for 2013/14

	£
Total income tax liability	12,100
Class 4 NIC	3,400
Tax deducted at source	(300)
Balance payable under self assessment	15,200

Two equal payments on account of 50% of the previous year's tax paid by self assessment are due on 31 January 2015 and 31 July 2015 in respect of 2014/15.

By 31 July 2015 Harold should have paid 100% of the previous year's tax due by self assessment, ie £15,200. As he has only paid £5,500 to date he should pay the balance of £9,700 on 31 July 2015 in order to minimise any interest charges.

25 B   £100

Ingrid should have submitted her 2013/14 tax return on 31 January 2015. A fixed penalty of £100 is due as it was submitted less than three months late.

The second payment on account was paid on 31 August 2014. The payment was due on 31 July 2014; however, no penalties are due on late payments on account.

Ingrid paid the final balancing payment for 2013/14 on 15 February 2015, 15 days late. Interest will be due but no penalty is due as the tax was not outstanding more than 30 days after the due date.

26 She wants HMRC to calculate her tax liability

    B   31 January 2016

She intends to calculate her own tax liability

    F   28 February 2016

The normal due date for filing a tax return where HMRC is to compute the liability is 31 October following the end of the tax year. However, where the notice to make a return is issued after 31 July following the end of the tax year, the deadline is extended to two months after the issue of the notice if HMRC are to calculate the tax liability, ie 31 January 2016.

The normal due date for filing a tax return where the taxpayer is to compute the liability is 31 January following the end of the tax year for a return filed online. However, where the notice to make a return is issued after 31 October following the end of the tax year, the deadline is extended to three months after the issue of the notice, ie 28 February 2016.

27 A   31 Jan 2016

The balancing payment is due by 31 January 2016.

    F   HMRC may amend the return until 10 June 2016.

This question is from the sample paper issued by the ICAEW.

28 B   19 April 2014

    D   6 July 2014

PAYE is payable 14 days after the end of each tax month. The last month of the tax year ends on 5 April 2014. It is therefore due by 19 April 2014.

P11D and P9D forms are due to be submitted to both HMRC and given to the employees by 6 July following the tax year end.

29 B   Form issued when an employee leaves employment

   D   End of year summary of tax and NICs per employee to be issued to each employee

      An end of year summary of tax and NICs deducted in the year per employee to be issued to each employee is a P60.

30 A   30% potential lost revenue

   C   £300 per return

      The fine for filing an incorrect P11D, with careless inaccuracies is 30% of potential lost revenue. The initial penalty for filing a late P11D is £300 per return.

31 B   31 May

32 A   P11D – 6 July 2015

   C   Final FPS – 19 April 2015

   F   P60 – 31 May 2015

      This question is from the sample paper issued by the ICAEW. It has been amended for changes to the PAYE rules.

33 C   31 December 2017

      A claim for 'overpayment relief' must be made within four years of the end of the accounting period.

34 A   31 August 2015

      HMRC has the right to amend a corporation return for obvious errors or omissions for nine months from the date the return is actually filed, ie from 30 November 2014.

35 D   30 April 2016

      Where a return is filed late, HMRC has the right to give notice of its intention to conduct an enquiry into a return for 12 months from the next quarter date of actual submission. The quarter dates are 31 January, 30 April, 31 July, and 31 October. The return should have been filed within 12 months of the period of account end, ie by 31 December 2014. As Azure plc filed its return late on 28 February 2015, the next quarter date is 30 April 2015, so the anniversary of that date is 30 April 2016.

36 C   1 January 2016

      A company which does not pay corporation tax at the main rate is required to pay its corporation tax liability within nine months and one day of its accounting period end. A company with taxable total profits of £1m for a 12 month accounting period and no associates will not pay corporation tax at the main rate.

37 B   £1,000

   C   5% of tax due in the return

      The return should have been filed within 12 months of the period of account end, ie 31 August 2014. As the return is more than six months late, there is an initial fixed penalty of £100 for a late return and then a daily fixed penalty of £900 (£10 per day for a maximum of 90 days) once the return is three months late.

      As the return is now more than six months but less than one year late (it is currently ten months late), a tax geared penalty also applies. This is 5% of the tax due in the return.

38 D   £1,000 fixed penalty and 5% tax-geared penalty

   F   10% of tax outstanding.

      There is a 5% penalty if tax is not paid by the filing date and a further 5% if tax is unpaid three months after the filing date. There would be a further 5% penalty if tax was unpaid nine months after the filing date (31 January 2015)

39   C   Blunt Ltd – 31 March 2021

     E   Jim – 31 January 2021

         A company must keep its records for six years from the end of the accounting period. An individual must keep his business records for five years from 31 January following the tax year.

         This question is from the sample paper issued by the ICAEW.

40   A   Y/e 30 September 2013 – By 1 July 2014

     F   Y/e 30 September 2014– By instalments

         A company does not have to pay tax by instalments in the first accounting period that it is a main rate company provided its augmented profits ≤ £10,000,000

41   D   Nil

         The failure to register is not deliberate so there is a maximum penalty of 30% of potential lost revenue.

         Edmund registers within 12 months of when he should have and pays the tax due at that time. Therefore the penalty will be nil.

42   C   Daniel's full income tax return for 2014/15 received on 4 July 2015 should be submitted to HMRC by 31 October 2015, if Daniel wants HMRC to calculate the tax

     E   Frank Ltd's P11D's for 2014/15 should be submitted to HMRC by 6 July 2015.

         A VAT return must be submitted electronically seven calendar days after the last day of the month following the end of the return period , ie 7 April 2015.

         The partnership income tax return has to be submitted online by the later of 31 January following the tax year or three months from receiving the return – in this case by 3 February 2016.

         Eagle Ltd has one year from the end of the period of account to submit its corporation tax return, ie by 31 December 2015.

43   D   £38.40

         The penalty is 3% × unpaid tax = £38.40. This is the third default in the penalty notice period.

44   C   £200

         There would have been an initial penalty of £100 for the first filing of a late VAT return for the quarter to 30 April 2013 and this would have started a twelve month penalty period, running from the due date 7 June 2014. The first default within the penalty period results in a penalty of £200. The penalty period is extended to 7 December 2015.

45   B   £1,080

         The maximum penalty for a 'not deliberate' failure to notify is 30% of potential lost revenue of £10,800.

         As HMRC has been notified of the need to register the penalty can be reduced. The tax was unpaid for more than 12 months so the penalty can be reduced to a minimum of 10% of £10,800, ie £1,080.

46   A   Careless

     F   0% of potential lost revenue

         The error is careless. The disclosure to HMRC is unprompted and therefore the penalty can be reduced to 0% of potential lost revenue.

47   D   A correction cannot be made in the next return because the error exceeds £50,000.

         The reporting error threshold is the higher of £10,000 and 1% of turnover (£5.6m @ 1% = £56,000), subject to an overall maximum of £50,000.

         The error must therefore be disclosed to HMRC rather than adjusted for in the next return.

48 C   £2,100

Ethel has made a deliberate but not concealed error. The maximum penalty would be 70% of potential lost revenue.

Ethel's prompted disclosure means that the penalty can be reduced to 35% of potential lost revenue.

Potential lost revenue is:

£15,000 × 40% = £6,000

Therefore 35% × £6,000 = £2,100

49 D   Insufficient funds to pay the tax due

50 D   As this is the third late payment in the tax year the penalty is 1% of the tax unpaid.

51 A   True – A taxpayer may appeal against an information notice

    D   False – A taxpayer has no right of appeal against an inspection notice

PRINCIPLES OF TAXATION

Tax Tables FA2014

The tax tables reproduced on the following pages are identical to the tax tables you will be given in the exam. Familiarise yourself with the content so that you know what you need to learn and what you can access in the exam from the tax tables.

In the actual exam, for ease of use on screen, your tax tables are divided into sections in accordance with the five key syllabus areas. You will find that for each question in the actual exam you will only be able to access the part of the tax tables relevant to that part of the syllabus. This is to minimise the amount of time you will need to spend scrolling through the tax tables.

Questions on each syllabus area will therefore only be able to access the pages of the tax tables as follows:

• Administration	pages 185-189
• Income tax & NIC	pages 190-191
• Capital gains	page 192
• Corporation tax	page 193
• VAT	page 194

SYLLABUS AREA: ADMINISTRATION

SUBMISSION DATES

Submission dates for 2014/15 personal self-assessment tax returns

Return filed online	Later of: • 31 January 2016 • 3 months from the date of issue of return
Paper returns: [1]	Later of: • 31 October 2015 • 3 months from the date of issue of return

(1) If HMRC is to calculate tax due on a paper return, the filing date is the later of 31 October 2015 and two months from the date the notice to make a return was issued.

Submission dates for corporation tax returns

Must be filed by 12 months from the end of the period of account

Submission dates for PAYE information: Real Time Information

Information	Filing date
Full Payment Submission (FPS)	On or before the day the employee is paid
P60 (to employees)	31 May following the tax year end
P9D and P11D	6 July following the tax year end

PAYMENT DATES

Payment dates for income tax

Payment	Filing date
First interim payment [1]	31 January in the tax year
Second interim payment [1]	31 July following the tax year end
Balancing payment	31 January following the tax year end

(1) Interim payments are not required if:

- The tax paid by assessment for the previous year was less than £1,000; or
- More than 80% of the tax liability the previous year was collected at source.

Payment dates for capital gains tax

Capital gains tax is payable by 31 January following the tax year end

Payment dates for corporation tax

Corporation tax	Nine months and one day after the end of an accounting period
Corporation tax by instalments	The 14th day of months 7, 10, 13 and 16 counted from the start of a 12-month accounting period

Payment dates for VAT

Online return	Due date
Electronic payment	7 calendar days after the last day of the month following the end of the return period
Direct debit payment	Collected automatically 3 working days after electronic payment due date

SYLLABUS AREA: ADMINISTRATION

MAIN PENALTY PROVISIONS

Individuals: penalties

Offence	Maximum Penalty
Failure to notify chargeability by 5 October following tax year end	See below: penalties for failure to notify
Late return	See below: penalties for late filing of returns
Late payment of income tax or capital gains tax: [(1)] • Unpaid 30 days after payment due date • Unpaid 6 months after payment due date • Unpaid 12 months after payment due date	 5% of tax unpaid Further 5% of tax unpaid Further 5% of tax unpaid
Failure to keep and retain tax records	See below: record keeping penalties

(1)   Late payment penalties do not apply to payments on account

Companies: penalties

Offence	Maximum Penalty
Failure to notify commencement of the first accounting period within 3 months of start	Fixed rate penalty not exceeding £300
Failure to notify chargeability within 12 months of end of accounting period	See below: penalties for failure to notify
Late return	See below: penalties for late filing of returns
Late payment of corporation tax: • Unpaid at filing date • Unpaid 3 months after due filing date • Unpaid 9 months after due filing date	 5% of tax unpaid Further 5% of tax unpaid Further 5% of tax unpaid
Failure to keep and retain records	See below: record keeping penalties

PAYE: penalties for late returns/ submissions

Forms/ submissions	Initial delay	Continuing delay	Delay exceeds 12 months
Final Full Payment Submission (FPS) [(1)]		£100 monthly per 50 employees	Further penalty not exceeding 100% of the income tax and NICs payable for the year of assessment but not paid by 19 April (22 April for electronic payments) following the end of the tax year
P9D and P11D	£300 per return	£60 per day	

(1)   Late submission penalties do not apply to late submission of in-year FPS

PAYE: penalties for late payment

Penalties for late payment of in-year PAYE depend on the number of defaults in the tax year	No of late payments	% of tax unpaid[(1)]
	1st	nil
	2nd, 3rd & 4th	1%
	5th, 6th & 7th	2%
	8th, 9th & 10th	3%
	11th or more	4%
Where a penalty has been imposed and the tax remains unpaid at 6 months		5%[(2)]
Where a penalty has been imposed and the tax remains unpaid at 12 months		5%[(2)]

(1)   The percentage penalty is applied to the total amount that is late in the relevant tax month. However, no default is charged in respect of the first late payment in the year.

(2)   The 6 month and the possible further 12 month penalties are in addition to the initial penalty for late payment

SYLLABUS AREA: ADMINISTRATION

VAT: penalties

Offence	Maximum Penalty
Failure to notify liability for registration or change in nature of supplies by person exempted from registration	See below: penalties for failure to notify
Failure to keep and retain tax records	See below: record keeping penalties

VAT: penalty for late filing of VAT returns

	Monthly returns	Quarterly returns
Initial penalty	£100	£100
Further late returns within penalty period (expires 12 months after the most recent late return)	1st to 5th late return: £100 6th and subsequent late return: £200	1st late return: £200 2nd late return: £300 3rd or subsequent late return: £400
Further penalty if return still unfiled after 6 months	Further penalty of 5% of the tax due (minimum £300)	
Further penalty if return still unfiled after 12 months	Further tax geared penalties apply (minimum £300): • 100% of tax due if deliberate and concealed • 70% of tax due if deliberate but not concealed • 5% of tax due in all other cases	

VAT: penalty for late payment of VAT

Amounts in respect of	Monthly returns	Quarterly Returns
Penalty for default within penalty period	1st, 2nd or 3rd default: 1% 4th, 5th or 6th default: 2% 7th, 8th or 9th default: 3% 10th or subsequent default: 4%	1st default: 2% 2nd default: 3% 3rd or subsequent default: 4%
After 6 months	Further penalty of 5% of tax still unpaid	
After 12 months	Further penalty of 5% of tax still unpaid	

VAT errors

An error made on a VAT return can be corrected on the next return provided it was not deliberate and does not exceed the greater of:

• £10,000 (net under-declaration minus over-declaration); or
• 1% x net VAT turnover for return period (maximum £50,000)

Alternatively, a 'small' error which is not deliberate may be corrected via the submission of form VAT652. Errors which are not 'small' or errors which are deliberate should be notified to HMRC on form VAT652.

SYLLABUS AREA: ADMINISTRATION

PENALTIES FOR INCORRECT RETURNS

The penalties are a percentage of the potential lost revenue

Reason for penalty	Maximum penalty	Minimum penalty with unprompted disclosure	Minimum penalty with prompted disclosure
Careless action	30%	Nil	15%
Deliberate but not concealed action	70%	20%	35%
Deliberate and concealed action	100%	30%	50%

PENALTIES FOR FAILURE TO NOTIFY

Failures to notify chargeability to tax, or liability to register for tax that leads to a loss of tax will result in a penalty. The penalties are a percentage of the potential lost revenue.

Reason for penalty	Maximum penalty	Minimum penalty with unprompted disclosure		Minimum penalty with prompted disclosure	
Deliberate and concealed action	100%	30%		50%	
Deliberate but not concealed action	70%	20%		35%	
		>12mths	<12mths	>12mths	<12mths
Any other case	30%	10%	Nil	20%	10%

PENALTIES FOR LATE FILING OF RETURNS

The penalties for late filing of a return are as follows:

Offence	Maximum Penalty
Late return	Immediate £100 fixed penalty
Return more than 3 months late	Daily fixed penalties of up to £10 per day for maximum 90 days
Return more than 6 months but less than 12 months late	Further, tax geared penalty of 5% of tax due (minimum £300)
Return 12 months late	Further, tax geared penalties apply (minimum £300) : • 100% if deliberate and concealed[1] • 70% if deliberate but not concealed[1] • 5% in all other cases

(1)   These tax geared penalties are reduced for disclosure as per penalties for incorrect returns.

RECORD KEEPING PENALTY

Offence	Maximum Penalty
Failure to keep and retain tax records	£3,000 per tax year/accounting period

SYLLABUS AREA: ADMINISTRATION

INCOME TAX RATES	2014/15
Starting rate for savings income only	10%
Basic rate for non-savings and savings income only	20%
Basic rate for dividends	10%
Higher rate for non-savings and savings income only	40%
Higher rate for dividends	32.5%
Additional rate for non-savings and savings income only	45%
Additional rate for dividends	37.5%

Basic rate band	£1 – £31,865
Higher rate band	£31,866 – £150,000
Starting rate band for savings income only	£1 – £2,880

INCOME TAX RELIEFS	2014/15
Personal allowance	£10,000
– individuals born after 5 April 1938 but before 6 April 1948	£10,500
– individuals born before 6 April 1938	£10,660

CGT RATES	2014/15
Gains falling within the remaining basic rate band	18%
Gains exceeding the basic rate band	28%

CORPORATION TAX RATES	FY 2014	FY 2013
Main rate	21%	23%
Small profits rate	20%	20%
Profit limit for small profits rate (lower limit)	£300,000	£300,000
Profit limit for marginal relief (upper limit)	£1,500,000	£1,500,000
Standard fraction	1/400	3/400

	2014/15		
NIC CLASS 1 CONTRIBUTIONS	**Annual**	**Monthly**	**Weekly**
Lower earnings limit (LEL)	£5,772	£481	£111
Primary and secondary earnings thresholds (PT & ST)	£7,956	£663	£153
Upper earnings limit (UEL)	£41,865	£3,489	£805
Employment allowance (per year, per employer)	£2,000		
Class 1 Primary contributions on earnings between PT & UEL	12%		
Class 1 Primary contributions on earnings above UEL	2%		
Class 1 Secondary contributions on earnings above ST	13.8%		
Class 1A contributions	13.8%		

NIC CLASS 2 CONTRIBUTIONS	2014/15
Normal rate	£2.75 pw
Small earnings exception	£5,885 pa

NIC CLASS 4 CONTRIBUTIONS	
Annual lower profits limit (LPL)	£7,956
Annual upper profits limit (UPL)	£41,865
Percentage rate between LPL & UPL	9%
Percentage rate above UPL	2%

VAT	
Standard rate of VAT	20%
Reduced rate of VAT	5%

ICAEW – CERTIFICATE LEVEL

TAX TABLES FA2014

SYLLABUS AREA: INCOME TAX & NIC

INCOME TAX RATES

	2014/15
Starting rate for savings income only	10%
Basic rate for non-savings and savings income only	20%
Basic rate for dividends	10%
Higher rate for non-savings and savings income only	40%
Higher rate for dividends	32.5%
Additional rate for non-savings and savings income only	45%
Additional rate for dividends	37.5%

Basic rate band	£1 – £31,865
Higher rate band	£31,866 – £150,000
Starting rate band for savings income only	£1 – £2,880

INCOME TAX RELIEFS

	2014/15
Personal allowance	£10,000
– individuals born after 5 April 1938 but before 6 April 1948	£10,500
– individuals born before 6 April 1938	£10,660
Married couple's allowance (relief is given at 10%)	
– At least one spouse/partner born before 6 April 1935	£8,165
– Maximum income before abatement of relief	£27,000
– Minimum allowance	£3,140

COMPANY CARS, VANS AND FUEL

Company cars

Cash equivalent 0% of list price for cars with no CO_2 emissions
5% of list price for cars emitting 1-75g/km
11% of list price for cars emitting 76-94g/km

12% of list price for cars emitting 95-99g/km
Increased by 1% per 5g/km over the 95g/km relevant threshold
Capped at 35% of list price

3% supplement on all diesel cars (subject to 35% cap)

Private fuel provided for company car

£21,700 x company car %

Van scale charge

£3,090 if van has CO_2 emissions

Additional £581 if private fuel provided for the van

Neither charge applies if either CO_2 emissions are nil or there is insignificant private usage

CAPITAL ALLOWANCES

First year allowances available

100% on new energy saving plant or machinery
100% on new and unused low emission cars ie not more than 95g/km CO_2 emissions
100% on new and unused zero emissions goods vehicles

Annual investment allowance

£500,000 of expenditure incurred by any business on certain plant and machinery between 6 April 2014 and 31 December 2015.

Writing down allowances

18% pa in the main pool

ICAEW – CERTIFICATE LEVEL

TAX TABLES FA2014

SYLLABUS AREA: INCOME TAX & NIC

NATIONAL INSURANCE CONTRIBUTIONS

NIC CLASS 1 CONTRIBUTIONS

		2014/15		
		Annual	**Monthly**	**Weekly**
Lower earnings limit (LEL)		£5,772	£481	£111
Primary and secondary earnings thresholds (PT & ST)		£7,956	£663	£153
Upper earnings limit (UEL)		£41,865	£3,489	£805
Employment allowance (per year, per employer)	£2,000			
Class 1 Primary contributions on earnings between PT & UEL	12%			
Class 1 Primary contributions on earnings above UEL	2%			
Class 1 Secondary contributions on earnings above ST	13.8%			
Class 1A contributions	13.8%			

NIC CLASS 2 CONTRIBUTIONS

	2014/15
Normal rate	£2.75 pw
Small earnings exception	£5,885 pa

NIC CLASS 4 CONTRIBUTIONS

Annual lower profits limit (LPL)	£7,956
Annual upper profits limit (UPL)	£41,865
Percentage rate between LPL & UPL	9%
Percentage rate above UPL	2%

PAYE CODES

L   tax code with basic personal allowance

P   tax code with full personal allowance for person born after 5 April 1938 but before 6 April 1948

Y   tax code with full personal allowance for those born before 6 April 1938

K   total allowances are less than total deductions

ICAEW - CERTIFICATE LEVEL

TAX TABLES FA2014

SYLLABUS AREA: CAPITAL GAINS

	2014/15
Annual exempt amount	£11,000
Gains falling within the remaining basic rate band	18%
Gains exceeding the basic rate band	28%
Basic rate band	£1 – £31,865

SYLLABUS AREA: CORPORATION TAX

Financial year	FY 2014	FY 2013
Main rate	21%	23%
Small profits rate	20%	20%
Profit limit for small profits rate (lower limit)	£300,000	£300,000
Profit limit for marginal relief (upper limit)	£1,500,000	£1,500,000
Standard fraction	1/400	3/400

Marginal relief

$$(\text{Upper Limit} - \text{Augmented Profits}) \times \frac{\text{TTP}}{\text{Augmented Profits}} \times \text{Standard Fraction}$$

CAPITAL ALLOWANCES

First year allowances available

100% on new energy saving plant or machinery
100% on new and unused low emission cars ie not more than 95g/km CO_2 emissions
100% on new and unused zero emissions goods vehicles

Annual investment allowance

£500,000 of expenditure incurred by any company on certain plant and machinery between 1 April 2014 and 31 December 2015.

Writing down allowances
18% pa in the main pool

SYLLABUS AREA: VALUE ADDED TAX

Standard rate		20%
Reduced rate		5%
Annual registration limit	From 1 April 2014	£81,000
De-registration limit	From 1 April 2014	£79,000
VAT fraction (standard rated)		1/6

Cash accounting	**From 01.04.07**
	£
Turnover threshold to join scheme	1,350,000
Turnover threshold to leave scheme	1,600,000

Annual accounting	**From 01.04.06**
Turnover threshold to join scheme	1,350,000
Turnover threshold to leave scheme	1,600,000

Flat rate scheme	**From 04.01.11**
Annual taxable turnover limit (excluding VAT) to join scheme	150,000
Annual total income (including VAT) to leave scheme	230,000

REVIEW FORM – PRINCIPLES OF TAXATION: Question Bank

Your ratings, comments and suggestions would be appreciated on the following areas of
this Question Bank

	Very useful	Useful	Not useful
Number of questions in each section	☐	☐	☐
Standard of answers	☐	☐	☐
Amount of guidance on exam technique	☐	☐	☐
Quality of marking guides	☐	☐	☐

	Excellent	Good	Adequate	Poor
Overall opinion of this Question Bank	☐	☐	☐	☐

Please return completed form to:

The Learning Team
Learning and Professional Department
ICAEW
Metropolitan House
321 Avebury Boulevard
Milton Keynes
MK9 2FZ
E learning@icaew.com

For space to add further comments please see overleaf.

REVIEW FORM (continued)

TELL US WHAT YOU THINK

Please note any further comments and suggestions/errors below.